Contents

Introduction 3

I. Doctrine 7

II. Security 16

III. The Soviet System 30

IV. Conclusions 40

Notes 44

Deterrence, War-fighting and Soviet Military Doctrine

INTRODUCTION

For more than a decade Western academic and government specialists have debated the significance of Soviet military doctrine and its implications for Western security. Controversy has centred on whether Soviet leaders accept such Western concepts as deterrence based on 'Mutual Assured Destruction' (MAD) or whether they reject these concepts and seek to acquire a nuclear war-fighting and war-winning capability, either to dissuade an opponent from starting a war or, in the event that war does occur, to be able to fight and win it. Although this debate was confined initially to the pages of academic journals and the reports of various institutes, by the late 1970s it had engaged the attention of political leaders in the United States and the Soviet Union and had become a factor in the foreign policies of both countries.

The emergence of Soviet (and by implication American) doctrine into the political forum was nowhere more evident than in the propaganda war conducted by the two powers in 1981. In the autumn of that year, the US Secretary of Defense, Caspar Weinberger, issued a pamphlet outlining the growth of Soviet military power in which a prominent place was assigned to an explication of Soviet doctrine.[1] The Soviet Government countered with two pamphlets, one of which took the unusual step of disavowing former tenets of Soviet doctrine and claiming that American analyses were based on outdated writings of the early 1960s.[2] More recently, the late President Leonid Brezhnev injected the controversy over doctrine into his message to the United Nations Special Session on Disarmament. Brezhnev claimed that renouncing the first-use of nuclear weapons proved the purely 'defensive' nature of Soviet doctrine. He charged that an American refusal to take a parallel step would demonstrate that the US not the Soviet Union was wedded to the concept of nuclear 'first strike'.[3]

This recent high-level controversy has its origins in a debate which has developed in the West over the last ten years. On the one side, analysts such as Fritz Ermarth, Benjamin Lambeth and Richard Pipes posited a clear contrast between Soviet and American attitudes towards deterrence and the question of whether fighting and winning a nuclear war is possible. In the Soviet Union, they argued, no political or military leader publicly claimed that the search for protection against nuclear attack would make attack itself more likely, or that deterrence would be undermined by unilateral Soviet acquisition of a pre-emptive first-strike capability. Soviet negotiators in the Strategic Arms Limitation Talks (SALT) showed no interest in a dialogue with the United States on the question of strategic 'stability', nor did the Soviet Union refrain – as the

US had for a period – from increasing the accuracy of its warheads to prevent them from becoming or being seen as 'counterforce' weapons.[4] According to these analysts, all indications were that the Soviet Union was determined to achieve a superiority in both offensive and defensive weapons which would enable it to fight and win a nuclear war.

In opposition to this view, analysts such as Raymond Garthoff dismissed Soviet doctrinal statements about war-fighting and war-winning. He suggested that such statements were intended only for sustaining morale in the armed forces and in no way reflected real Soviet thinking on these matters. On the basis of mostly indirect evidence, Garthoff and others argued that the Soviet leaders in fact did accept a mutual deterrence relationship with the United States as desirable. Soviet adherence to the Anti-Ballistic Missile (ABM) Treaty of 1972, they contended, as well as occasional Soviet statements to the effect that nuclear war would be 'mutual suicide', suggested that the Soviet Union was not embarked on a quest for a war-winning capability in a potential nuclear conflict.[5] At a minimum, these analysts saw a continuing 'debate' in the Soviet Union, in which some individuals rejected the war-fighting rationale and adhered more closely to American views about the impossibility of fighting a nuclear war.

Insofar as there were any winners in this debate, clearly the 'hawks' – those who claimed that the Soviet leaders rejected Western concepts of deterrence – gained the upper hand. A virtual industry burgeoned in American universities and research institutes in which numerous authors sought to prove the fundamentally alien character of Soviet doctrine. These authors allowed Soviet doctrine to speak for itself – by marshalling quotations from classified and unclassified sources that left little doubt that Soviet and American doctrines were based on fundamentally different values and perceptions.[6] Recent defensiveness in the USSR about the content of Soviet doctrine is testimony to the success of Western specialists in popularizing an especially disturbing assessment of Soviet thinking about nuclear war.

As is evident from the discussion so far, the debate on doctrine was structured for the most part by a rigid deterrence/war-fighting dichotomy, with the US said to be committed unequivocally to the former, and the USSR to the latter. There is a large element of truth in this generalization, but, like all such generalizations, it simplifies and tends to cloud reality. In light of the growing recognition in the West that Soviet and American doctrines are different, the time has come for analysts to shift the focus of the debate away from this somewhat artificial dichotomy towards some of the ambiguities and subtleties in Soviet thinking.

As a first step towards such a shift, the deterrence/war-fighting dichotomy itself may be usefully re-examined. Is it in fact as absolute as many analysts have suggested? Two sets of facts call into question the absoluteness of this dichotomy. First, while war-fighting has attracted Soviet more than American strategists, it does have a certain appeal in the US – as the domestic dissatisfaction with MAD clearly indicates. Second, though mutual deterrence is rejected by most Soviet writers, these same writers are quite vague in explaining precisely how the Soviet Union expects to 'win' a nuclear war.

While attention has focused on the Soviet rejection of MAD, it is less frequently recalled that American acceptance of MAD was never total, nor was its dominance of US doctrine anything but short-lived. The practice of drawing iron-clad distinctions between deterrence and war-fighting can be traced back to the mid-1960s and to US Defense Secretary Robert McNamara. Even then there was a considerable disjunction between US declaratory policy and targeting doctrine, because throughout this period the US retained a significant capability to strike military (i.e. counter-force) targets and planned in war to do so. Prior to this period, American civilian and military leaders, including McNamara himself, generally assumed that nuclear weapons would be used in a counterforce mode against Soviet strategic forces and other military targets.[7] By 1970, the Nixon Administration was explicitly challenging even MAD as declaratory policy on the grounds that it left the President 'with the single option of ordering the mass destruction of enemy civilians, in the face of the certainty that it would be followed by the mass slaughter of Americans'.[8] The drift away from MAD continued with the 1974 Schlesinger Doctrine and the institution in that doctrine of a policy of 'limited nuclear options'.[9] Continued American interest in the counterforce side of nuclear warfare was evident in the Carter Administration's Presidential Directive (PD)59, and, subsequently, in the policies of the Reagan Administration which has shown a revived interest in civil and ballistic-missile defence.[10]

In moving away from MAD and re-emphasizing the military utility of nuclear weapons, successive US administrations have claimed to be interested primarily in strengthening deterrence, which remained the over-riding objective of US strategic forces. The emphasis was always on how credible war-fighting options would strengthen deterrence, rather than on war-fighting for its own sake. While many in the US began to recognize the inadequacy of MAD as a strategy, few saw any real possibility of returning to the position of near invulnerability which the US had once enjoyed.

Nevertheless, MAD was abandoned, making all the more puzzling the fact that, by the early 1970s, it had become a standard by which analysts judged both Soviet and American doctrine. The 'doves' – those who accepted MAD – combed the Soviet literature for evidence that the Soviet leadership also accepted this particular concept. Failing, for the most part, to find such evidence, they were left vulnerable to charges that, because the Soviet leadership rejected American doctrine, the USSR thought it could 'fight and win a nuclear war'. The 'hawks', in contrast, were quick to characterize the Soviet Union as aggressive because it did not reach the standard embodied in the concept of MAD, even though, when it came to US forces, the 'hawks' themselves rejected MAD. In other words, MAD had ceased to be anything but an arbitrary standard and one which had less and less to do with the doctrine, force posture or research and development (R&D) programmes of either the United States or the Soviet Union.

An unfortunate aspect of this analysis was the extent to which it was premised upon, and in turn fostered, an assumption that the strategic relationship between the US and the Soviet Union was straightforward and unambiguous, capable of being summarized in a set of propositions called 'doctrine'. One side could have the 'right' set of propositions, the other the 'wrong' set, and analysts had only to decide which side had which. Early in the SALT process, American officials set out to 'educate' Soviet leaders into abandoning their presumably erroneous doctrine and into moving closer to American views. By the end of the 1970s, the reverse had occurred. Observers such as Colin Gray could note that the United States was abandoning its mistaken views and adopting a doctrine which had much in common with Soviet thinking.[11] What the controversy over the 'right' and 'wrong' views of deterrence and war-fighting failed to consider, however, was a third possibility: that doctrine could mask ambiguity, contradiction and uncertainty about nuclear weapons, thereby rendering dubious the very notion of a 'right' or 'wrong' strategic doctrine and its exclusive possession by one government or one country.

In moving beyond the deterrence/war-fighting dichotomy, this Paper will explore the hypothesis that both Soviet and American doctrines are at best imperfect attempts to come to grips with dilemmas inherent in the nuclear competition which cannot be reduced to, or resolved by, a simple set of propositions. These dilemmas arise from the fact that nuclear weapons have three different, and in many ways contradictory aspects, which are reflected in the doctrine of a state. These aspects are: deterrent; war-fighting; and political.

In order to disentangle these aspects of the nuclear weapons competition, the Paper will examine three broad topics. First, it will reconsider the notion of 'doctrine'. Doctrine provides a link between certain 'objective' military realities – in this case the existence of nuclear weapons with particular characteristics – and a political system which inevitably reflects 'subjective' values and uncertainties. One should expect to find some relationship between the nature of a political system and the way in which it understands and manages nuclear competition. Second, the Paper will consider the problem of security in the nuclear age and how it is reflected in doctrine. It will argue that security is a relative concept that is best understood in terms of a continuum between minimum and maximum levels, rather than in terms of an absolute choice between security through deterrence and security through war-fighting. The Paper will argue that, while Soviet leaders do understand and value deterrence as a 'minimum' guarantee of their security, they seek to go beyond this minimum level and to maximize Soviet security by the acquisition of war-fighting capabilities. Third and finally, the Paper will analyse certain basic features of the Soviet system which may motivate the apparent drive to maximize Soviet security through the pursuit of war-fighting capabilities.

I. DOCTRINE

Contradictions in the nuclear competition

The military doctrine of both the US and the Soviet Union (or indeed of any state) must contend with the fact that nuclear weapons have different and often contradictory aspects, depending upon the context in which they are viewed. These aspects, as noted in the Introduction, can be termed deterrent, war-fighting and political. In regard to the first, the bluntness of nuclear weapons makes them inherently unsuited for use as a military instrument. Their ability to kill very large numbers of people and thus provoke a retaliatory strike is *prima facie* an argument for not using nuclear weapons. Recognition of this, now reinforced by predictions of a 'nuclear winter', constitutes the essence of deterrence. Indeed the proponents of MAD attempted to accentuate this aspect of nuclear weapons so as to minimize the likelihood of deterrence ever failing.

This purely deterrent aspect of nuclear weapons seems to have been understood by both sides very early in the nuclear era. On 8 December 1953, in an address to the UN, President Eisenhower spoke of the consequences of nuclear war, which he saw as no less than 'the possibility of civilization destroyed . . . and the condemnation of mankind to begin all over the age-old struggle upward from savagery'.[12] As if in reply to, and in tacit agreement with the American President, some three months later Soviet Premier Malenkov stated that nuclear war would be a 'holocaust' that would mean 'the destruction of world civilization'.[13] Despite the fact that Malenkov's unequivocal statement was later disavowed by the Soviet leadership, other Soviet comments do indicate an awareness of the catastrophic consequences of nuclear war.

Second, although it was widely recognized that nuclear weapons have little political utility, they remain weapons nonetheless. They are likely to be used if deterrence fails, and military organizations on both sides develop plans for their use. From the onset of the atomic era, the very lethality of the nuclear weapon encouraged military and civilian thinkers to search for ways to blunt the effects of a direct nuclear attack. This was particularly important for the Soviet Union, which for the first few years of the post-war era possessed no nuclear deterrent and thus had to rely for protection entirely on 'damage limitation' measures. Damage limitation concepts thus entered early into the Soviet calculus and were adopted later in the United States. As schemes for protection against nuclear attack (once both sides had acquired nuclear weapons) began to centre on preemptive nuclear strikes against the opposing side's nuclear forces, the prospect of counterforce warfare entered the US-Soviet strategic rivalry. It has remained a factor in this rivalry ever since. However much one may fear for the future of deterrence and the prospects of a destabilizing counterforce arms race, it could be argued that damage limitation and counterforce are almost inevitable concomitants of the (equally inevitable) countervalue aspects of nuclear weapons.

Third, nuclear weapons, though unusable as military instruments, are paradoxically important political symbols which confer certain distinct advantages on their possessors. These advantages, moreover, seem to accrue not merely in a general way, but rather precisely in proportion to the size and sophistication of the various national arsenals. Conditions like 'inferiority', 'parity' or 'superiority' have become politically significant, even though the sheer unusability of nuclear weapons would seem to argue against the political relevance (indeed the military relevance also, assuming that deterrence holds) of even quite large disparities between the various national arsenals. In addition, 'extended deterrence' and Soviet efforts, short of war, to undermine it are complex political phenomena whose relationships to US and Soviet nuclear capabilities are impossible to pin down precisely, yet nonetheless exist.[14]

US and Soviet efforts to deal with contradiction
Like their American counterparts, Soviet leaders formulate opinions and make statements about these three aspects, even though inherent contradictions exist between them. Not surprisingly, the United States and the Soviet Union deal with these contradictions in ways that reflect their respective political systems.

In the United States, individuals, institutions and at times political parties appear to seize upon one level or another of the nuclear problem to the exclusion of others. Protagonists thus tend to discuss nuclear matters in a way that minimizes attention to inherent ambiguities and contradictions. Some supporters of arms control, for example, have fastened upon the need to preserve mutual vulnerabilities in order not to obscure the fundamental fact that nuclear weapons *cannot* be used to achieve political ends. In doing so, they have ignored the pressures towards damage limitation and counterforce inherent in the nuclear rivalry with the Soviet Union. They have also ignored the political implications of the nuclear balance and of its perceived shifts. For their part, proponents of war-fighting do not appear to have appreciated adequately the uncertainties attending *any* attempt to use nuclear weapons, or the political dangers of talking about their use.

Whereas in the US the inherent contradictions tend to be debated openly among different institutions or political forces – thus giving the spurious impression that there is a 'right' answer to the nuclear dilemma – in the Soviet Union these contradictions are incorporated, unresolved, into doctrine. In the Soviet Union, as in the United States, the nuclear problem is thus reshaped in the image of the political system itself. In the US, the openness of society and the need to debate publicly matters of policy virtually compel policy advocates to transform contradictions inherent in the possession of nuclear weapons into 'error' that resides in the mind of the political and policy opponent. In the Soviet Union, in contrast, the closed nature of society and the party-governmental monopoly on 'truth' generally lead the government-controlled media not to assign 'error' or 'truth' to divergent views expressed within the system but simply to subsume these views within a seemingly monolithic and all-embracing body of official doctrine which, as can be seen upon closer inspection, merely incorporates and papers over contradictions that in the US are argued out in public. In the United States, confusion and disagreement about nuclear weapons are widely dispersed throughout the polity; in the Soviet Union, they are systematically incorporated into a body of statements which is 'official' and authoritative, but at the same time often vague and self-contradictory.

In addition, American governments frequently revise their declaratory nuclear doctrine, as different aspects of the nuclear competition come to the attention of policy-makers. Often shifts in doctrine from one administration to another or even between different phases of a single administration exaggerate the degree of change at the level of targeting, force planning and the setting of R&D priorities. While the American political system makes for frequent change in declared doctrine, the Soviet system appears to do the opposite. Soviet governments revise doctrine very slowly, if at all.

While the mutual renunciation of comprehensive ABM systems by both the US and the Soviet Union, for example, would be a significant political, military and technological event that one might expect to see reflected in military doctrine, Soviet writings largely ignore the ABM Treaty of 1972. As Thomas W. Wolfe has observed, there is virtually no difference between Marshall Grechko's discussion of strategic defence in 1975, and an earlier discussion which appeared prior to the conclusion of the ABM Treaty.[15] Some analysts have argued, with some justification, that the immobility of Soviet doctrine can be attributed to deep-seated national proclivities – to a 'national style' or a 'strategic culture'[16] – which makes for a lag in adjustments to technological change. Others suggest, however, that this immobility arises precisely because the doctrine is vague, contradictory and contains a marked gap between theory and reality. Much as Marxist-Leninist ideology as a whole is broad and vague enough to accommodate a variety of policies, Soviet military doctrine – which is, after all, a sub-branch of Marxist-Leninist theory – allows Soviet military and political leaders latitude in shaping policies.

Implicit in this interpretation of Soviet doctrine is the view that it is *not*, contrary to what is frequently asserted in the West, perfectly consistent and that it does not offer superior insights into the dilemmas of the nuclear age. Moreover, because inconsistencies in Soviet doctrine are readily apparent, the real task for Western analysts is not to continue to contrast Soviet and American doctrine, but to separate the contradictory strands within Soviet doctrine itself, and to analyse which strands reflect military policy, which are primarily political, and which, if any, are likely to respond to changes in American policy.

Inconsistencies in Soviet doctrine
In this light, it is worth examining some of the major inconsistencies in Soviet doctrine. First, on the purely military level, there is a tendency in

Soviet writings to treat *intentions* and *capabilities* as interchangeable. When V.D. Sokolovskii, for example, proclaims that 'it is necessary to develop and perfect the instruments and methods of combat with a view to *attaining victory over the aggressor, above all in the shortest possible time*',[17] he clearly implies that the Soviet armed forces do not yet have this capability. It must be 'developed'. His statement is thus one of intent. Yet it contains no assessment of precisely what additional forces will be required to turn the intention into a capability. Moreover, in prescribing the actual course of a future war, he writes as if this capability had been achieved already. Sokolovskii gives no indication of what a 'second best' course of action might be. If war were to break out tomorrow, and the Soviet Union had not yet acquired a war-winning capability, how would it behave? Much of Soviet doctrine, insofar as it assumes capabilities that simply do not exist, avoids the most difficult military questions. It does so by pushing war off into a hypothetical future in which the Party has 'solved' the very questions which in the West are deemed almost insoluble. This vagueness about capabilities – in marked contrast to the ruthless scrutiny which US capabilities undergo in public debate[18] – permits Soviet doctrine to gloss over the contradiction between the war-fighting (use) and the deterrent (non-use) aspects of nuclear weapons.

Second, on the political level Soviet writings contain an apparent contradiction between military and political elements. In the Soviet Union, writers use the term 'military doctrine' to encompass both the political and military aspects of doctrine, with the latter subordinated to the former. Doctrine is held to be 'scientific' and class-based (Marxism-Leninism being the 'science' of class conflict), and applies not to individual military units but to the state as a whole and its official policy.[19] Doctrine in Soviet parlance is thus by definition political. While many critics of US policy and doctrine have been quick to admire Soviet policy-makers as thorough-going Clausewitzians who successfully integrate military and political elements in their doctrine, there are numerous contradictions between military and political objectives which are simply glossed over in Soviet doctrine. As military analysts, Soviet writers have long recognized the inherent advantages of striking first against a nuclear opponent. Soviet writings are replete with references to the need to break up an enemy's attack by 'by dealing him in good time a crushing blow'. Yet on the political level, Soviet policy consistently claims that the Soviet Union is firmly opposed to the concept of nuclear first-strike or indeed the first use of nuclear weapons in any theatre. Soviet writers circumvent this contradiction by arguing that Soviet doctrine (i.e. the policy of the state) is invariably defensive, even though Soviet strategy (i.e. the policy of the armed forces once war has been thrust upon the state) may be offensive. As the recent embarrassment of Soviet officials indicates, however, in practice the Soviet Union has great difficulty convincing the outside world of the relevance of this distinction.

In countering charges that Soviet doctrine is aggressive, Soviet commentators have complained that Western analysts confuse Soviet strategy and tactics with Soviet doctrine. According to one military writer:

> Some Western military figures and propagandists, grossly distorting the essence of our military doctrine, try to 'prove' that it cannot be defensive since the Soviet Army and Navy are equipped with powerful offensive weapons, including strategic weapons, and are allegedly being trained in predominantly offensive actions.
>
> The absurd and ill-intentioned nature of these allegations is easily spotted with the naked eye. The socio-political essence and content of any state's military doctrine are determined not by arms and their qualities and potential, but by the policy of the state, and the military and political aims it sets for itself and its armed forces.[20]

While there is a grain of truth in the Soviet distinction (just as one must acknowledge a distinction between the intentions of the US President and Congress and the operational plans of the US military), ultimately one must reject it as irrelevant. To accept the view that Soviet 'doctrine' is by definition peaceful, irrespective of the 'strategy' and behaviour of its armed forces, is tantamount to accepting a Marxist-Leninist view of the world and to abandoning any critical assessment of Soviet thought. For those unable to accept this view, Soviet 'doctrine' will continue to display glaring contradictions between its political and its military aspects. (In the present context, then, 'doctrine' will be used in a Western rather than a Soviet sense and thus will encompass elements that Soviet writers would claim properly belong to 'strategy'.)

Brezhnev's 'no-first-use' pledge brought into even sharper focus the contradiction between the state's peace-loving protestations on the political level and its parallel claim that the Soviet Union can guarantee its security by military means alone if necessary. This tension is evident in an authoritative article by former Defence Minister Ustinov, which first praises Brezhnev's initiative, but then proceeds to make a veiled allusion to Soviet war-fighting plans thereby indirectly negating the no-first-use pledge itself:

> Washington and the other NATO capitals should clearly realize that the Soviet Union, in renouncing the first use of nuclear weapons, is also denying the first use of nuclear weapons to all those who are hatching plans for a nuclear attack and calculating on a victory in a nuclear war. The state of the military potentials and military technological capabilities of the sides is such that the imperialist forces will not succeed in attaining military superiority *either at the stage of preparations for nuclear war or at the moment when they try to start such a war.*[21]

Had Ustinov simply stated that the 'imperialist forces will not succeed in attaining military superiority ... at the stage of preparations for nuclear war', observers in the West might have concluded that the Soviet Defence Minister was expressing doubt about the advisability of all efforts to acquire war-fighting capabilities. In adding the phrase, '*or at the moment when they try to start such a war*', however, Ustinov seems to be expressing the familiar Soviet sentiment that deterrence is not assured, that the 'imperialists' could conceivably delude themselves into thinking that they could fight and win a nuclear war, provided they struck first, and finally, that if they did so, the USSR would have to be prepared. Ustinov's reference to the possibility of such attempts, as well as to their inevitable failure, suggests that he is encouraging the Soviet armed forces to acquire capabilities to limit the damage and perhaps even 'win' in the event of nuclear conflict. To the degree that all such attempts must, given existing technologies, depend on some kind of first-strike capability, the implications of Ustinov's statement run counter to Brezhnev's unequivocal declaration of 'no-first-use'.

This 'doctrine/strategy' distinction which the USSR maintains simply introduces into Soviet military thinking all the characteristics peculiar to Marxism-Leninism as a general system of thought. This has both advantages and disadvantages. On the positive side, it allows for infinite flexibility in propaganda and diplomacy. On the negative side, however, it virtually blinds Soviet thinkers to important features of the nuclear competition with the United States. Except in the most oblique ways, Soviet writers are proscribed from discussing the impact of Soviet actions on the United States, or from considering such topics as intra-war negotiations or crisis stability. To discuss such topics would imply conferring upon the 'enemy' a degree of legitimacy of motives which cannot be countenanced by Marxism-Leninism. While there has been a tendency, particularly in the writings of US 'hawks', to praise the thorough-going (military) 'realism' of Soviet writers and to contrast this realism with the 'intellectualizing' of American (civilian) theorists,[22] it is probably more correct to ascribe at least some of this 'realism' to the inhibiting Marxist-Leninist framework which constrains Soviet analysts from exploring freely many important aspects of the super-power nuclear competition.

Deception in Soviet doctrine

The deterrence/war-fighting dichotomy which structured Western discussions of Soviet doctrine inevitably led to an emphasis on the literal reading of Soviet texts. The issue was whether or not Soviet doctrine contained a 'blueprint' for preparing for and waging a nuclear war. If, however, Soviet doctrine is taken out of the deterrence/war-fighting context and seen as responding to the three different aspects of nuclear weapons mentioned before – deterrent, war-fighting and political – then one should expect considerably less clarity than the term 'blueprint' implies. One would expect, as has been suggested already, a certain amount of internal inconsistency and even a degree of deception, as Soviet spokesmen seek to smooth over those contradictions.

Recent studies take a different approach than earlier works, many of which devoted considerable attention to the role of deception and political bluff in doctrine. In *Strategic Power and Soviet Foreign Policy*, Arnold

Horelick and Myron Rush argued that Soviet statements, at least at the level of the top leadership, often served to deceive.[23] By comparing Soviet statements with what could be determined subsequently about Soviet defence policies at the time the statements were made, the authors concluded that Soviet leaders often said precisely the opposite of what they must really have thought. Herbert Dinerstein, as will be seen below, demonstrated that, during the Khrushchev period, there was usually an inverse correlation between Soviet rhetoric about the danger of nuclear war and the actual level of international tensions.

Drawing upon the works of Horelick and Rush, Dinerstein and others, George Quester later offered an explanation as to why deception was practised by Soviet (and Chinese) leaders in the public exposition of strategic doctrine. In his article 'On the Identification of Real and Pretended Communist Military Doctrine', Quester distinguished four stages in the evolution of Soviet declaratory positions, each of which was adapted to the strategic arsenal of the Soviet Union at the time and calculated to maximize its deterrent and political value.[24]

In the first stage, which lasted from 1945 until the early 1950s, the Soviet Union possessed no nuclear deterrent of its own. A logical response to this situation was to depreciate altogether the utility – counterforce and countervalue – of nuclear weapons and to claim that victory in war could still be assured by a reliance on the Soviet Union's own main advantage: its large conventional land force. This was the public stance adopted by Josef Stalin. In retrospect, of course, it became clear that Stalin had fully appreciated the significance of the atomic bomb and had ordered feverish efforts to be made to break the American monopoly. According to defectors and various other corroborating sources, not only did Stalin seek an atomic bomb, but as early as 1947 he had approved programmes designed to give the Soviet Union a capability to deliver the weapon against US territory.[25] Another indication of Stalin's true feelings was provided several years later by the Yugoslav Communist, Milovan Djilas, who revealed that Stalin had confided to him privately his appreciation of the potential importance of the new American device.[26]

With the acquisition of a modest nuclear capability, the USSR then moved into a stage in which its interests were better served by a new rhetorical posture. At this point, Soviet leaders had reason to exaggerate, rather than depreciate, as previously, the countervalue aspects of nuclear weapons, while continuing to deny their military, counterforce utility. This posture would accomplish two objectives at once: it would help to deter a pre-emptive attack by a still militarily-superior United States, while at the same time convincing the US that the Soviet leaders, now possessing nuclear weapons, understood their power and would not use them recklessly. In short, the new Soviet attitude towards nuclear weapons was intended to foster doubt in the US about both the need for and the feasibility of a preventive war against the Soviet Union.

As the Soviet Union began to stockpile nuclear weapons and more sophisticated delivery systems, its rhetorical stance shifted again.

Possessing far more of a genuine deterrent at this time, the USSR no longer needed to worry about a preventive war, which by then was far too risky for an American President even to contemplate, and Soviet leaders then began to talk freely about the military uses of nuclear weapons. A new emphasis on the military utility of rockets, in particular, was politically valuable in that it undercut the willingness of third countries to host US forces, and in particular American strategic bombers. By claiming an ability to destroy selected military targets, and even by cultivating a certain ambiguity as to whether the Soviet Union might not under certain circumstances launch a pre-emptive nuclear attack, Khrushchev probably hoped to bring pressure to bear on these countries. He was able to do so now without significantly increasing the possibility of a US attack on the Soviet Union. While Soviet doctrine thus began to discuss counterforce options, it continued to emphasize the countervalue aspects of nuclear weapons, at least as they applied to smaller countries which, as Khrushchev frequently stressed, could be 'wiped out' in a nuclear war.[27]

In addition to these three stages, Quester saw a fourth possible stage in the evolution of Soviet doctrine – one that would be appropriate for a situation in which the USSR had achieved marked superiority over the US. In this hypothetical stage it could be expected that the USSR would once again depreciate the countervalue effects of nuclear weapons, so as to create doubts in the US about the effectiveness of its own deterrent. At the same time, Soviet doctrine would emphasize the counterforce possibilities of its own nuclear weapons, again with the objective of undermining American faith in the US deterrent and presumably American resolve in a crisis. In effect, such a declaratory policy would claim a Soviet war-fighting capability, but do so largely in order to influence the perceptions of outside powers for political gain. Soviet statements would not necessarily serve as an operational or planning guide for the Soviet military.

The USSR never achieved the degree of nuclear superiority that would allow it to exploit such a doctrine. Indeed, with the collapse of the 'missile gap' in 1961, the Soviet Union apparently fell back to a 'stage two' declaratory policy rather than advancing confidently to 'stage four'.[28] In the early 1960s, however, Soviet commentators spoke enthusiastically about the prospects for ABM systems, which, if developed and deployed successfully, might have placed the USSR in a position where it would want to adopt a doctrine which would emphasize Soviet invulnerability and thereby cast doubt on the effectiveness of the American deterrent.[29]

Limited nuclear war

Another area in which Soviet declaratory doctrine can be seen to serve mainly deceptive purposes is the issue of limited nuclear war. There is no *a priori* reason why, after an exchange of nuclear strikes either in Europe or between the homelands of the two main nuclear powers, one side could not back down or negotiate to terminate hostilities. Nor is there any historical evidence to suggest that the USSR, for ideological or political reasons, is unable to conduct limited conventional war, as it did in the attack on Poland in 1939, the Finnish War of 1939–40, the war on Japan in 1945, or, more recently, in the war in Afghanistan.[30] Nonetheless, for at least the first decade and a half of the nuclear age, Soviet declaratory doctrine consistently rebuffed American suggestions that nuclear war could be limited in any way, insisting that any use of nuclear weapons would lead to general nuclear war, the collapse of 'imperialism' and probably hundreds of millions of casualties.

The Soviet insistence on the impossibility of limited nuclear war – as opposed to the unlikelihood or undesirability acknowledged by Western commentators[31] – was based on a desire to enhance deterrence and to reap political benefits rather than on an objective, 'scientific' assessment of what might be the actual course of events in case of war. Possessing smaller and less accurate nuclear forces for most of the nuclear era, the Soviet Union would inevitably be disadvantaged in a limited nuclear war. It therefore had to put the US on notice that it would not fight such a war by American rules. In addition, there were compelling political reasons why the Soviet Union would want to rule out the possibility of limited nuclear war, since doing so would undermine the credibility of American weapons in Europe and of extended deterrence.

At least in regard to war in the European theatre, then, the familiar Western assertion that Soviet doctrine treats these weapons as military instruments while US doctrine treats these weapons as unusable (suitable only for deterrence) is not strictly true. When it suits Soviet interests, Soviet doctrine will stress the uselessness of nuclear weapons by retreating into rhetoric about 'global holocaust' and the like. In contrast, it has been the US which has been more willing to talk realistically about a limited use of nuclear weapons for specific military purposes, notably to stop a conventional attack by Soviet forces.

As Soviet forces grew in size and sophistication, the Soviet military began to reassess the prospects for limited nuclear war in Europe.[32] Soviet political leaders and most military writers continued to disparage talk of limited nuclear war, but the absolute taboo on the mention of its mere possibility was lifted in the early 1960s. The most plausible reason for this shift is quite simple: the capabilities and hence the objective interests of the Soviet Union had changed.

II. SECURITY

Minimum and maximum security objectives
If, as has been suggested, Soviet doctrine does contend with the different aspects – deterrent, political and military – of nuclear weapons, a prime objective for research ought to be to try to identify what criteria the Soviet leadership uses to make judgments about the relative importance of and the inter-relationship between these different aspects. In the West, much of the public controversy about nuclear strategy is really about how one should judge these same inter-relationships and relative priorities. Opponents of counterforce, for example, do not object to counterforce as such (for example, they do not argue that one kind of counterforce, namely targeting a missile silo, is *in itself* more objectionable than targeting Moscow). Rather they contend that counterforce options tend to be destabilizing for deterrence because such options could be used early in a crisis. Conversely, proponents of counterforce do not argue that fighting a nuclear war is *in itself* preferable to deterring one, but simply that deterrence is not assured. Thus fall-back strategies must be considered or, alternatively, they claim that a countersilo capability is the surest means of preserving deterrence.[33] Soviet leaders are unlikely to perceive these trade-offs in precisely the same way as their American counterparts. However, they are no doubt faced with the same problem of deciding whether or to what degree to assign priority to the purely deterrent, the political or the military aspects of nuclear weapons.

In light of the obvious role that deception plays in Soviet statements about nuclear matters, devising methods by which to distinguish the 'real' from the 'pretended' in Soviet statements is desirable though not always easy. To some extent, this analysis can be done retrospectively by contrasting Soviet statements with actual force procurement policies. By identifying the 'real' concerns and priorities of the Soviet leaders (reflected in actions), it should be possible to draw conclusions about the criteria Soviet leaders use in choosing between deterrence and war-fighting, or between the military and the political uses of nuclear weapons.

A number of general conclusions about the way in which Soviet leaders establish priorities do follow from the previous analysis of 'real' and 'pretended' Soviet doctrine. With regard to the military applications of nuclear weapons there is no clear pattern of consistent support – 'real' or 'pretended' – for either deterrence or war-fighting. Rather, there appears to be a mixed and often shifting pattern in which top political leaders have appealed to one or the other in response to changing conditions. Instead of the familiar deterrence/war-fighting dichotomy, what this pattern perhaps suggests is that top political leaders view Soviet security in terms of 'minimum' and 'maximum' levels. While they might prefer the latter, at times they are forced by circumstances to settle for the former.

While analysts have long spoken of Soviet foreign policy objectives in terms of minimum and maximum objectives, these categories have not been applied to strategic doctrine as such.[34] Doing so could prove useful in providing a context in which to interpret particular Soviet statements. As in foreign policy, attention to minimum or maximum objectives changes in response to changing conditions. In the early post-war period, for example, Soviet nuclear policy appeared to be motivated by a concern for securing a minimum deterrent. In contrast, the present nuclear balance indicates that the Soviet Union's minimum deterrent requirement is unlikely to be threatened seriously. Soviet doctrine is vague enough to accommodate the pursuit of these different objectives without itself undergoing revolutionary change. What changes is not the doctrine, but the emphasis that the regime places on different elements within the doctrine.

Doubtless the minimum requirement of Soviet declared doctrine has been to strengthen deterrence of an American attack on the Soviet Union, even if at times this meant opening up a large gap between private thoughts and public pronouncements. The classic example of this pattern of behaviour was Stalin's doctrine, which, as noted earlier, denied altogether the decisive role of nuclear weapons. With the growth of Soviet strategic power and the accompanying diminution of the possibility of preventive war by the United States, this minimum requirement was clearly met, and the strictly deterrent role of doctrine declined. In short, Soviet capabilities began to speak louder than Soviet words. With its insistence that *any* use of nuclear weapons would inevitably escalate to global nuclear holocaust, however, the USSR continued to rely on a 'pretended' doctrine to deter limited US military action.

On a few occasions Soviet leaders have fallen back to a greater emphasis on the purely deterrent aspects of nuclear weapons. In the present period, for example, and in much the way that Quester's analysis of past Soviet deception would predict, Soviet political leaders are responding to the US interest in limited nuclear options and to US plans to develop highly accurate counterforce weapons by once again stressing only the countervalue side of nuclear weapons and depreciating their military utility.

Another important aim of declared Soviet doctrine is political; public statements are made to influence outside political forces. These statements may either be intimidating, as when Khrushchev tried to frighten European countries from hosting US missiles and bombers, or soothing, as in the recent 'peace policy'. Khrushchev, in particular, seems to have tried to tailor his declaratory pronouncements to maximize the political utility of Soviet nuclear forces. By the early 1960s, he seemed less interested in claiming that Soviet nuclear forces were superior and that, as a consequence, they had a war-fighting advantage than in asserting – falsely – that the Soviet forces were equal to US forces and that this equality created a new political situation. Referring to the alleged parity in 1961, Khrushchev complained that in the West '... the necessary conclusions are not being drawn from this fact. With equal forces, there must be equal rights and opportunities ....'[35] Why then did Khrushchev use deception to try to achieve political parity, while following a defence policy which did not result in 'real' military parity – much less a genuine war-winning capability? Certainly at this point in Soviet history those who formulated declaratory doctrine were more preoccupied with the political value of nuclear weapons than with the purely military aspects of the US-Soviet nuclear competition.

Finally, the third function of declared Soviet doctrine – one that has received the most attention in the American debate – is to guide, educate and prepare the Soviet military to fight and win a nuclear war. Although war-fighting has remained a constant theme in Soviet doctrine, there is reason to suspect that war-fighting is the *least* important feature of Soviet declaratory doctrine, paradoxically because attaining a war-fighting capability is the *maximum* objective expressed in Soviet doctrine. War-fighting can be pursued only *after* a secure deterrent has been acquired (otherwise the opponent might be tempted to pre-empt before the Soviet Union realizes its more ambitious objectives), and, it could be argued, only in conjunction with an effective political strategy. While, as will be seen below, the Soviet armed forces have been preoccupied since at least 1955 with the problems of ensuring victory in nuclear war, the senior leadership has generally boasted of or called for war-fighting capabilities only to the extent that doing so could serve deterrent or political purposes.

When does the Soviet Union emphasize, either in its declaratory policy or in its force planning, the 'minimum' requirement of deterrence, and when does it emphasize the 'maximum' demands of war-fighting? Proceeding from the assumption that preparations for fighting a nuclear war should bear some relationship to beliefs about the likelihood of such a war, Soviet assessments of the prospects for war and the role that they play in the Soviet political system will be examined in the next section.

Soviet assessments of the war danger
For the United States and the Soviet Union, and indeed for any power, deterrence as a strategy makes sense only given a very high degree of confidence that this strategy will work, that the opponent is capable of being deterred. Even in the US, with its far greater proclivity to deterrence, this essential confidence can be undermined by political tensions. It is no accident that Defense Secretary McNamara's early interest in counterforce warfare and city avoidance coincided with the Berlin crisis,[36] or that the Schlesinger Doctrine of Limited Nuclear Options (LNO) followed shortly after the 1973 Middle East War and the accompanying nuclear alert.[37]

Turning to the Soviet Union, it is necessary to ask whether the perception of an increase in the possibility of war can lead to a shift from the deterrent elements in Soviet doctrine towards those relating to war-fighting. For a time, Khrushchev appeared to have decided on a minimum deterrent posture – one which, for purposes of saving resources for economic development, played down the war-fighting element which nonetheless remained present in Soviet doctrine.[38] He made similar kinds of choices with regard to *Sputnik*. As became evident to Western observers several years later, Khrushchev chose to exploit the political significance of Soviet advances in rocket technology by proclaiming the military significance of the *Sputnik* breakthrough, and then proceeding *not* to deploy a first-generation ICBM force.[39] Had Khrushchev's decision-making criteria been different, one could imagine a policy precisely the opposite of that actually adopted: strict secrecy about *Sputnik*, followed by rapid and secret application of the new Soviet technology in the creation of a first-generation ICBM force. Such a policy would have made far more sense in purely military terms had Khrushchev, for example, been planning to attack the US rather than merely challenging its self-confidence and undermining its international prestige. The counter-example to Khrushchev's behaviour was, of course, Stalin's handling of the initial development of nuclear weapons by the USSR. Soviet development of the bomb was not announced, and no attempt was made to exploit the Soviet breakthrough politically. In the Soviet view, war – perhaps in the form of a pre-emptive US strike – was, if not likely, at least possible. From the examples just given, it is evident that Soviet decision-making is heavily overshadowed by assessments of the likelihood of nuclear war. Many of Khrushchev's policies make sense only if it is assumed that he judged the likelihood of nuclear war with the US to be extremely low.

In light of the role that deception plays in Soviet declaratory doctrine, it is difficult to determine whether Soviet leaders believe that the likelihood of nuclear war is uniformly low and, if not, whether increases in the perceived probability of war lead to corresponding increases in the regime's emphasis on war-fighting. In attempting to analyse the relationship between Soviet assessments of the danger of war and Soviet strategic conduct, two possibilities present themselves. First, Soviet leaders occasionally perceive a 'real' rise in the possibility of war, and then adjust their doctrine to prepare for war-fighting. Second, Soviet leaders perceive the likelihood of war to be uniformly very low, but under certain circumstances, they 'pretend' to be frightened of the possibility of war, so as to justify their interest in acquiring war-fighting capabilities.

In the first instance, the fear of war would have to be regarded as a *cause* of Soviet interest in war-fighting. In the second instance, it would simply be an *instrument* serving to implement a policy the causes of which are to be found elsewhere. This section draws upon past Soviet handling of the war-danger theme to argue that the second of these two interpretations is the correct one. The implications of Soviet interest in war-fighting and the sources of this interest will be examined later.

Khrushchev's war-scare politics
As in many other areas of Soviet strategic thinking, the basic Soviet approach to this question was established in the early to mid-1950s and has not changed fundamentally since. After what appeared to be genuine controversy about whether or not there was a real danger of war, Soviet leaders generally concluded that there was not. In effect, they recognized,

as had Malenkov, that a situation of mutual deterrence existed. But instead of publicly admitting that the war danger was low, for various reasons Soviet leaders preferred to maintain a certain ambiguity on this issue, and to adjust assessments of the war danger to suit domestic and international political requirements.

Stalin's 'fatal inevitability of wars' was a doctrine whose very essence was the denial of the possibility of deterrence. War-fighting was the only security policy which could flow from such a doctrine. On the other hand, Malenkov's assessment that the imperialists could not gain from starting a nuclear war virtually precluded war-fighting altogether. What is noteworthy about the Soviet handling of this issue, at least after 1956, is the studious effort made to avoid choosing between Stalin's or Malenkov's clear-cut positions. Instead, there was a preference for an ambiguous stance which accommodated both the possibility that the US would be deterred and a parallel search for a war-fighting capability.

While Khrushchev was anxious to abandon a doctrine which seemed to preclude any policy but war-fighting, he was careful not to formulate a doctrine which would preclude any policy but deterrence. While he claimed that war was no longer 'inevitable', he did not say it was impossible. This rather truistic assessment allowed the Soviet leader considerable latitude in his assessment of war danger and hence considerable flexibility in his foreign and defence policies. This ambiguity has persisted in all subsequent Soviet thinking.

As early as March 1954, both Malenkov and Mikoyan (Deputy Chairman of the Council of Ministers) had stated that the Soviet Union possessed a secure deterrent capability and that therefore war (i.e. imperialist attack) was most unlikely. It is unclear whether Malenkov and his associates arrived at this conclusion based on an independent assessment of Soviet capabilities, or on an assessment of American behaviour, which was characterized by an increasingly sober view of the consequences of nuclear war and the virtual disappearance of talk of a preventive war against the Soviet Union. Whatever its causes, Malenkov's statement was so unambiguous that it had immediate policy implications. It meant that a relatively small Soviet force would be sufficient to maintain peace, and that resources could thus be diverted from the military to economic development. This adjustment of budgetary priorities entailed a shift of responsibility away from the military and heavy industry and towards light industry.[40]

Within weeks of delivering this optimistic assessment, Malenkov was under attack from a coalition led by Khrushchev, which accused the Soviet Premier of dangerous complacency in the face of imperialist attack. In stating unequivocally that the capitalists were engaged in the 'preparation of a new war', Khrushchev set in motion a process that forced Malenkov from power in January 1955. The initial Malenkov-Khrushchev dispute may have reflected the genuine disagreement which seemed to exist in the Soviet elite in the first years after Stalin's death about the prospects for war. After Malenkov's fall, however, assessments of the war danger had increasingly little to do with war itself and became mere instruments in internal political struggles.

Dinerstein has shown how, during the mid-1950s, Khrushchev several times whipped up and then quelled artificial war scares to consolidate or reconsolidate his domestic position. Despite his apparent concern about the danger of war, two years passed after Malenkov's demise in which there was virtually no mention in the Soviet political press of the danger of nuclear war. Throughout the summer and autumn of 1956, as tensions in Hungary and Poland mounted, Khrushchev and his associates played down the war danger. Only in early 1957 did Khrushchev generate a new war scare, the purpose of which appeared to be to help him to recoup his domestic position, which had been undermined by events in Eastern Europe. In February 1957 Khrushchev convened a Central Committee Plenum in which attention was drawn suddenly to the events of the previous autumn and the 'sharply increased ... threat of a new world war'.[41] Several weeks later Khrushchev suddenly changed his mind and pronounced, in response to no clearly identifiable international development, that the international situation had suddenly markedly improved.

As Dinerstein remarked in his analysis of Khrushchev's behaviour, 'it is difficult to resist the conclusion that in the Soviet Union the employment of such [war] alarms for minor purposes betokens a low estimate of the likelihood of war'.[42] 'It may be', he added, '... that the private and the public estimates of the likelihood of war seldom if ever coincide. When the danger is great, there is little disposition to cry wolf. When the danger recedes, there is a temptation to make domestic political capital out of the fear of war.'[43]

While subsequent political leaders have generally been less capricious than Khrushchev in manipulating assessments of the war danger, such assessments remain powerful instruments of political competition within the Soviet system. Khrushchev himself appears to have become embroiled in a dispute in which he was cast in the role of his previous opponent, Georgi Malenkov, and which may have contributed to his eventual fall from power. In his January 1960 report to the Supreme Soviet, Khrushchev claimed that surprise attack was no longer a feasible option for the United States, since the USSR would retain sufficient nuclear forces to launch a devastating retaliatory blow. In effect, Khrushchev was claiming that the USSR possessed a secure second-strike capability which guaranteed deterrence.[44] This formulation and the policy it supported came under heavy fire from the military, as was evident in the October 1961 speech of Marshal Malinovskii. The Soviet Defence Minister told the Twenty-Second Party Congress that the West was seriously preparing for a surprise nuclear attack on the USSR. He contended that Soviet forces needed to be improved so that they would be capable of 'breaking up the aggressive designs [of the enemy] by dealing him a crushing blow in time'.[45]

The war danger in the Brezhnev era

In the post-Khrushchev period there was (at least initially) less readiness on the part of the Soviet leadership to engage in war-scare politics. This reluctance persisted despite – or perhaps in part because of – the fact that the first years of the Brezhnev-Kosygin-Podgorny leadership were ones of increased tension with the United States. As the official *History of Soviet Foreign Policy* recalls: 'relations between the USSR and the USA deteriorated in 1964–1970'.[46] While throughout the Khrushchev period important Soviet pronouncements about the danger of nuclear war were made by Khrushchev himself (often in interviews with Western reporters),[47] the new 'collective leadership' adopted a lower profile, generally declining to make detailed pronouncements on strategic matters. Nor was there much discussion in the political press about nuclear war and the strategic competition with the US.

There are several reasons for the Brezhnev regime's reluctance to engage in war-scare politics. First, having been confronted in the Cuban missile crisis by a genuine possibility of war, the Soviet hierarchy was sufficiently shaken to abstain from public war talk for some time. Second, Brezhnev, Kosygin and the other Politburo members were committed to collective leadership and in consequence had less need to use the war-peace issue as an instrument in domestic political conflict. Third, debate about the likelihood of nuclear war may have faded from the Soviet political scene precisely because military and civilian leaders had reached a consensus on defence spending levels and essential long-term objectives, again lessening the need for war-scare politics.

In responding to the tensions of the mid-1960s, Soviet leaders continued to assert, in ritual fashion, that the objective of the Communist Party of the Soviet Union (CPSU) was to avert war, but that should war come, as Brezhnev claimed in his 1966 speech to the Twenty-Third Party Congress, 'the equipment of the Soviet troops is up to contemporary requirements, and their increased striking and fire-power are fully adequate for crushing any aggressor'.[48] The following year, Brezhnev proclaimed that in the event of war, Soviet forces could 'win a victory worthy of the Soviet people'.[49] These particular statements by Brezhnev were among the last by a top Soviet political leader calling for victory in nuclear war. From the late 1960s onwards, a constant low-level appeal to this danger seems to have been accepted as useful for the regime as a whole and for particular institutions within the Soviet system. On the political level, the appeal to the danger of war was linked to the conduct of the 'peace policy' initiated in 1971, and to the campaign for 'military detente' that began in 1973. On the military level, continued reference to the existential danger of nuclear war has sustained the military's claims on resources that might otherwise be undermined by detente and arms control.

In the 1970s, war-scare politics were virtually 'institutionalized' in Soviet politics. As a result of the increased stability of the Soviet system under Brezhnev and the trend towards domestic 'depoliticization' observed by many Sovietologists,[50] it became increasingly unlikely that a top political leader could be toppled – as was Malenkov – by implying that the Soviet Union might not survive a nuclear war. A more relaxed attitude prevailed which allowed for a division of labour in the treatment of the war-danger theme. Military writings continued to stress that the 'imperialists' were actively preparing for war, while top political leaders were equally glib in acknowledging – at least tacitly – Soviet vulnerabilities in referring to nuclear war as an act of 'mutual suicide' that would mean the 'end of civilization'.[51] As Brezhnev emerged as an active 'peace' campaigner in his own right, he revived to some extent Khrushchev's practice of making frequent public references to the possibilities for nuclear war, thus presenting himself as the world's guardian of peace.

Some evidence suggests that the stable pattern which had prevailed for much of the Brezhnev era began to break down towards the end of his rule and that war-scare politics were revived by organizations seeking to manipulate assessments of the likelihood of war to advance their claims to a share of resources. For example, Deputy Defence Minister and Chief of the General Staff N.V. Ogarkov, writing in the July 1981 issue of *Kommunist*, claimed that in the US 'direct war preparations are underway on a broad front' and that 'the material preparation of a new world war is being carried out'.[52] In February 1982 Ogarkov issued a booklet detailing plans for Soviet survival in face of a surprise US nuclear attack.[53] Among other things, Ogarkov called for an improvement in the ability of the USSR to mobilize its forces rapidly and to place its economy on a war footing. Ogarkov's statements may have had more to do with an attempt to shape domestic policy in accordance with the desires of the military than with his real assessment of the likelihood of nuclear war. Emphasis on US 'war preparations' both justifies high military expenditure and may help to combat the complacency and pacifism among Soviet youth which are known to concern the Soviet High Command. If the analysis offered here is correct, this new high-level attention to the danger of war has arisen in spite of – indeed has been made possible by – the fact that the Soviet leadership's 'real' assessment of the war danger is actually quite low.

As can be seen in the foregoing analysis, assessments of the likelihood of war or the possibilities of preventing war by deterrence are not 'objective' assessments in the Western sense. Rather, they are themselves factors in the domestic and international politics of the Soviet Union and thus subject to change. Domestically, arguments over whether deterrence is possible inevitably involve differing assessments of the nature of the capitalist enemy, which in turn touch upon the fundamental legitimacy – both domestic and international – of the Communist Party. Assessments of the likelihood of war are in practice usually determined by the Party's ideological and political needs and may often have little to do with 'objective' assessments of the prospects for war.

The experiences of Malenkov in 1954, of Khrushchev in the early 1960s and of the late Brezhnev period seem to indicate a general pattern. On the one hand, Soviet military and civilian thinkers do perceive a choice between a policy of simply maintaining a minimum deterrent against a US attack and one of seeking to go beyond this level to achieve a capability to survive and win a nuclear war. The former policy is relatively inexpensive and frees resources for economic growth, while the latter implies an almost open-ended claim on resources by the military. There is thus a strong economic rationale for deterrence. On the other hand, top political leaders who perceive the economic benefits of a minimum deterrent posture seem to expose themselves to charges that they are minimizing the likelihood of imperialist aggression and thus endangering Soviet security. For the Soviet regime in general, and for powerful groups within it, particularly the armed forces, the basic line remains, in effect: 'the imperialists would really like to launch a nuclear war, but so far they have not yet succeeded in finding a way to get away with it'. Whether or not anyone actually supports this position is almost beside the point. The most important consideration is that the continued propagation of this view serves both the overall foreign policy of the Soviet state (the 'peace policy'), and the interests of the most militaristic elements in the Soviet political system.

The war-fighting imperative

As a practical matter, deterrence in the nuclear age is relatively unproblematic. The statements by Eisenhower and Malenkov previously quoted suggest that a state of mutual deterrence probably existed as early as the mid- or even early 1950s – long before the complicated theorizing of the 1960s and 1970s arose in response to the problems of arms control, crisis stability, parity and so forth. However, as a theory, deterrence is fraught with difficulty. Since deterrence is a psychological phenomenon, its effectiveness depends upon the rationality and the value system of the opponent to be deterred. As a theory, deterrence does not provide any answer to the extra-rational problem of accidental war.

War-fighting presents precisely the opposite problem. In theory, winning a nuclear war is straightforward. Victory can be attained either by pre-emptively destroying the other side's nuclear weapons or by surviving a nuclear strike or by a combination of these. The practical implementation of this theory, however, presents problems.

The contradiction between the theoretical simplicities of war-fighting and its practical difficulties, or between the practical certainties of deterrence and its theoretical difficulties may be so obvious as to appear truistic. If so, however, this truism must be borne in mind in any discussion of Soviet doctrine. It is easier for Soviet writers to repeat the theoretical simplicities of war-fighting (and to neglect its practical difficulties) than to grasp the (theoretically difficult) nettle of deterrence. The obvious arguments against deterrence provide ammunition to those in the system who argue – either on principle or simply out of opportunism

– that the USSR must surmount these difficulties if it is to achieve 'real' security against an American attack.

Throughout the post-war period, some Soviet leaders and particular groups (such as the armed forces) have raised the spectre of war (of imperialist attack) in order to advance claims on resources needed to acquire a war-fighting capability. While war-scare politics have been successful, for the most part, in supporting high defence expenditures and in preventing the adoption of an 'image of the enemy' which would undermine the CPSU's basis of legitimacy, it is not at all clear how highly civilian and military leaders assess the prospects for achieving a genuine, high-confidence, war-fighting capability. While the Soviet military have followed the maxim that 'more is always better', there is reason to doubt that they have concluded that, when it comes to winning a nuclear war, 'more is enough'.

THE PERIOD FROM 1945 TO 1953

In the 1945–53 period, the war-fighting imperative manifested itself mainly in claims by the Soviet military that the USSR could absorb American nuclear attacks and, at the same time, occupy Western Europe by conventional means and thus deny American access to overseas bases on the Soviet periphery. War-winning, in short, consisted of overcoming the atomic bomb by conventional means. It is difficult to determine, even in retrospect, to what extent Soviet military thinkers actually believed these claims and to what extent they advanced them either to please Stalin or simply to deter the US and its West European allies or to create anxieties in the minds of both Americans and West Europeans.

While Stalin lived, doctrine had to uphold the correctness of his World War II decisions and exempt him from blame for the disastrous unpreparedness of the country in the face of German attack in 1941. According to Stalin's formula of the 'permanently operating factors', victory in war would be determined by 'the stability of the rear, the morale of the army, the quantity and quality of divisions, the armament of the army, and the ability of the army commanders'.[54] As Dinerstein has remarked, Stalin's formula was 'so truistic as to be almost devoid of meaning'.[55] It did, however, stress the social and economic character of war, and reaffirmed the Marxist-Leninist contention that victory in war would inevitably go to the superior social system. It also stressed the Soviet Union's historic advantages, a large army and population, and claimed that the US, like Germany, would be unable to derive a permanent advantage from such 'transitory' factors as surprise and pre-emption, even if these were to take a nuclear form.

Unfortunately for Soviet military planners, Stalin's military thinking was at best ill-suited and at worst inimical to intelligent thinking about the military problems raised by the appearance of the atomic weapon. While arguably the most pressing problem of the nuclear age had become that of surprise attack, the distinctive feature of Stalin's doctrine was precisely its contention that surprise, while it could be tactically significant, was strategically irrelevant. Certainly as long as the Soviet Union did not possess its own nuclear weapons, this systematic denigration of the atomic bomb served something of a deterrent purpose and sustained Soviet political prestige. By late 1953, however, it was becoming increasingly clear to at least some military officials that a doctrine which for deterrent and political purposes denied a decisive role to nuclear weapons (thus denying the possibility of US nuclear blackmail against the Soviet Union), was not useful for preparing the Soviet military and civilian leadership for nuclear war, should one occur. What was needed – and was now possible – was a doctrine which integrated nuclear weapons into Soviet war-fighting plans. In effect, there was a growing incompatibility between deterrence as a minimum security objective and the maximum objective of war-fighting. With the former fairly secure, a few Soviet military figures began thinking about the latter.

THE PERIOD FROM 1953 TO 1955

The open challenge to Stalinist doctrine came in late 1953, with the publication of an article by Major General Talenskii in *Voennaia mysl* (*Military Thought*).[56] Talenskii's article evoked an enormous response in the armed forces and sparked a debate which lasted until April 1955. The actual progress of this debate has been described in a number of excellent studies,[57] and need not be recounted in detail in this context. In essence, however, what emerged from the debate was a consensus that a 'military-technical revolution' had occurred with the appearance of atomic weapons and their delivery systems, and that Soviet doctrine and planning had to adjust to this revolution. Unlike the proponents of the earlier Stalinist view, which stressed that the outcome of war would be determined by the social order of the competing states, Talenskii emphasized the importance of combat itself and claimed that the same rules of warfare applied for both sides. Whereas Stalin's doctrine assumed that victory for the Soviet Union was inevitable owing to its superior social system, Talenskii at least implied that the Soviet Union could be defeated in war if it did not understand and adapt to the changed nature of war itself. Ironically, only by discussing in realistic terms the possibility of Soviet *defeat* in nuclear war could Talenskii encourage his colleagues to think realistically about *victory* in such a war.

Despite the seeming finality of Talenskii's conclusions, the debate of the early 1950s left certain ambiguities which still cast a shadow over Soviet doctrine. The debate involved two questions, only one of which was fully resolved. First, there was the question of whether nuclear weapons had altered the nature of war fundamentally, thus rendering irrelevant concepts like the 'permanently operating factors'. Although there was some opposition from the ground forces, Talenskii won an unambiguous victory on this score. It became official Soviet doctrine that a 'revolution' had occurred in military affairs.

However, given that nuclear weapons *had* fundamentally altered the nature of warfare, a second question arose as to whether war-fighting was still feasible at all, and if so by what means. Some Soviet writers seemed compelled to conclude that the answer to the first question predetermined the answer to the second: if war was fundamentally changed, this change consisted precisely in the fact that war was no longer 'winnable'. Other Soviet writers rejected this interpretation and argued that the revolution in military affairs did not negate the goal of victory itself, but simply called for new means by which to achieve it. Faced with this ambiguity, powerful groups in the Soviet Union, including the armed forces and, in particular, the Strategic Rocket Forces, have always had an interest in maintaining that it is the second of these interpretations which guides the policy of the top political leadership.

The 1953-4 debate remains the watershed event in the development of Soviet strategic thought. The entry on 'Military Strategy' by the then Chief of the General Staff, Marshall Ogarkov, appearing in the 1979 edition of the *Soviet Military Encyclopedia*, distinguishes only two periods in the history of post-World War II military strategy: 1945-53 and post-1954.[58]

The centrality of the 1953-4 shift suggests that, from the point of view of the Soviet armed forces, the particular problems posed by technological developments, shifts in the military balance, arms control – in short all the events of the post-1954 period – are, while not unimportant, clearly subordinate to the *fundamental* problem posed by the appearance of the atomic weapon and its integration into the armed forces. Moreover, in 1979, Ogarkov clearly stated that this 'problem' is in fact nothing less than that of 'victory in nuclear war':

> Soviet military strategy proceeds from the view that should the Soviet Union be thrust into a nuclear war then the Soviet people and their Armed Forces need to be prepared for the most severe and protracted trial. The Soviet Union and the fraternal socialist states will be in this case, in comparison to the imperialist states, in possession of definite advantages, the established just goals of the war, and the advanced nature of their social and state systems. This creates for them the objective possibility of achieving victory. However, for the realization of this possibility there is the necessity for timely and comprehensive preparation of the country and the Armed Forces.[59]

THE PERIOD SINCE 1955

As numerous analysts of Soviet doctrine and strategy have pointed out, since 1955 there have been continuous efforts to acquire the capabilities to support a war-winning strategy.[60] In 1955, after Khrushchev had come to power in part by exploiting the war-danger theme, the Soviet Union embarked on a programme to acquire the intermediate-range ballistic missiles (IRBM), necessary to destroy pre-emptively the American bomber force (based mainly in Europe and North Africa) which then formed the backbone of the US nuclear force.[61] Throughout this period, most Soviet military literature (and Khrushchev himself) boasted of the superior war-fighting virtues of the missile over the bomber. In the early 1960s, with the development of the US strategic triad, the task of acquiring the forces needed for pre-emption became much more difficult, but was nonetheless undertaken by Khrushchev and the subsequent regime. US intelligence officials now conclude that as early as 1962 or 1963 the Soviet Union began a project aimed at acquiring a highly accurate missile force to destroy US ICBM on the ground.[62] In addition, during the late 1950s and early 1960s, as the US began to deploy *Polaris* submarine-based missiles, the Soviet navy shifted its priorities away from countering US carrier groups and towards anti-submarine warfare (ASW) capabilities.[63]

The Soviet approach to war-fighting was always guided (although not entirely dominated) by the principle that in the nuclear age offence enjoys a fundamental advantage over defence. Although in theory a nuclear war could be won by a combination of active and passive defences, in practice no one has yet devised the defensive systems which could counter a nuclear attack effectively, President Reagan's Strategic Defense Initiative notwithstanding. Soviet doctrine, then, has always emphasized the need to frustrate pre-emptively any attack against the Soviet Union. As all three editions (1962, 1963, 1968) of Sokolovskii conclude:

> The imperialists are preparing an offensive war against our country, a war of total destruction and mass annihilation of population using nuclear weapons. Therefore, they must be countered with decisive active operations by our armed forces, mainly with crushing nuclear blows from strategic weapons. Only in this way can we curb the imperialist aggressors, foil their criminal plans, and defeat them. Under present conditions, strategic defence and then a counter-offensive cannot assure the attainment of these decisive war aims.[64]

Sokolovskii adds that 'defence as an enforced temporary type of military operation will have a place in a future war', and that 'our troops should study and master defence....'[65] Soviet military planners have, in fact, grafted defensive, damage limitation measures onto their pre-emptive strategy, and have received high-level support for these efforts.[66] The major impetus behind the current Soviet civil defence programme came from Brezhnev in 1966, who endorsed it in his speech to the Twenty-Third Party Congress.[67] Throughout the 1960s, the Soviet Union also maintained a large ABM research programme and, as recently as 1970, some Soviet military writers were still claiming that the USSR had systems 'capable of reliably striking both enemy aircraft and missiles'.[68] However, as Soviet willingness to accept an ABM Treaty later seemed to confirm, Soviet military thinkers remained wedded to the view that the most effective defence against nuclear attack was offence.

Still, many in the armed forces continued to doubt the feasibility of a war-fighting strategy. According to Thomas Wolfe, between 1965 and 1967 there was yet another replay in the specialized military literature of this old debate.[69] By that time even the more 'hawkish' participants in the debate seemed readier than in the 1950s to acknowledge the problems associated with nuclear war-fighting. Those who argued that victory was possible admitted that the present state of technology and the current balance of forces afforded little prospect for achieving a war-winning capability in the near term, but that the future might bring technological breakthroughs which would enable the Soviet Union to enhance its security dramatically. Those who held out this possibility were clearly attempting to influence the spending priorities of the new leadership in Moscow, so as to ensure that large resources would continue to be available for the long-term build-up of Soviet forces and for the R & D from which technical breakthroughs might result.

Each time the USSR moved towards a war-winning capability, it not only underestimated the inherent technical difficulties involved (i.e. in countering existing US forces), but it also failed to appreciate that this effort would provoke American counter-efforts, which often resulted in a diminished rather than an enhanced level of security for the Soviet Union. Soviet efforts in the 1950s to threaten the US bomber forces led to American development of an invulnerable strategic 'triad'. By the late 1970s, the Soviet effort to threaten this triad not only stimulated the US to deploy new and less vulnerable systems, but also to upgrade its own counterforce capabilities. In the 1980s, the US is considering the strategic defence option, at least partly in response to the growth of Soviet offensive capabilities.

Despite the mixed record of Soviet efforts to achieve – at enormous cost – a high-confidence war-fighting capability, any future Soviet leadership is likely to respond, as in the past, to pressures that militate in the direction of a war-fighting strategy. Moreover, while the weaknesses of the theory of deterrence have been as frequently exposed in the US as in the USSR, only the Soviet system has shown a special responsiveness to arguments against deterrence. The next Chapter will consider the features of the Soviet political system which may account for this receptiveness.

III. THE SOVIET SYSTEM

Marxism-Leninism and the Soviet conception of security
Even a cursory view of Soviet history demonstrates the progress that the Soviet regime has made from a position of extreme vulnerability – when it seemed that the survival of the 1917 Revolution would be determined by the actions of the German proletariat – to near invulnerability which came with the achievement of super-power status. In the nuclear age, the Soviet Union has made a similar progression from a stage when it could not deter an American nuclear attack, to one where deterrence is virtually guaranteed by the condition of mutual assured destruction. The question naturally arises as to whether there is some stopping point at which the dependence on external deterministic forces (the policies of other states, unforeseen events and limits on resources) and reliance on voluntary efforts (by military means, by forming alliances, etc.) has shifted far enough in the direction of the latter to permit the Soviet state to *feel* 'secure'.

One of the distinctive features of Soviet doctrine and behaviour over the past decade is the apparent disinclination to acknowledge that there is such a 'stopping point' beyond which further 'voluntaristic' efforts to enhance security may prove unnecessary or even counterproductive. Certainly strategic parity did not mark this point, as the West once hoped. As Wolfe concluded in 1975:

> both political leaders and military professionals still seem deeply reluctant in security matters to part with the belief that they can successfully structure their own security, and equally reluctant to trust someone else to help look out for it .... [B]oth leadership groups continue to regard as inherently suspect any effort to construct a stable military-strategic relationship with the capitalist adversary on the basis of each side's being solicitous of the other's security concerns ....[70]

Insights into Soviet thinking about the relative role of voluntaristic and deterministic forces in assuring security can be gleaned from Soviet interpretations of past events. At any moment in its history the Soviet Union tends to exaggerate its own strengths – its own voluntaristic ability to shape its destiny – even though Soviet leaders in private may be less confident and may be making furious efforts to overcome existing but unacknowledged weaknesses. Only in retrospect is it acknowledged that security was in fact preserved by deterministic elements over which *at the time* the Soviet Union had less than complete control. When the US had a complete nuclear monopoly, Soviet commentators adopted the line that the 'atomic bomb is a paper tiger' and declared that the USSR by its own efforts could defeat even a nuclear attack. Retrospective assessments are far less confident. According to the standard Soviet diplomatic history, the Soviet Union's first nuclear explosion 'put an end to a difficult and dangerous period in international life when the USA pursued an aggressive policy founded on its monopoly of nuclear weapons and tried to impose its will on many countries'.[71]

In explaining why the US did not use the atomic bomb in this period, this source mentions nothing about Soviet military capabilities, but points to splits among US leaders and most importantly, to 'the mobilization of world democratic opinion against US policy'.[72] Soviet assessments of the Cuban missile crisis are also characterized by an unusual emphasis on factors largely outside the control of the Soviet leadership. The same diplomatic history states that war was averted in 1962 not by Soviet power but by the 'wisdom' of the leaders concerned.[73]

The intent of such retrospective acknowledgments of vulnerability is to congratulate the Party for the wisdom it showed in preserving and strengthening Socialism and the Soviet people from the aggressive intentions of the 'Imperialists'. While Soviet leaders thus recognize that the USSR has become more secure, no gain in security is ever attributed to moderation in the West. On the contrary, the West's aggressive intent is emphasized so as to heighten the Party's achievement in 'foiling' these intentions.

This way of interpreting the past is yet another disturbing indicator of the degree to which the USSR insists on identifying real security only with unilateral efforts. By the same token, however, Soviet acknowledgment of such vulnerabilities, even if only in retrospect, casts doubt on the Western assertion that Soviet leaders understand deterrence *only* in terms of an effective war-fighting capability. Clearly Soviet leaders appreciate the barriers against Western use of nuclear weapons, including the possession of a secure Soviet 'second strike capability'. By the late 1950s, Khrushchev seems to have concluded that the US would not, for both political and military reasons, attack the Soviet Union, although he remained preoccupied with the possibility of 'accidental' war and of a 'madman' coming to power in the US who could not be deterred. Post-Khrushchev regimes have been similarly concerned that deterrence may not be enough, as, for example, in 1975 when Boris Ponomarev warned of the dangers of a 'fascist' takeover of a Western country armed with nuclear weapons.

Depending upon one's perspective, one can either be encouraged that Soviet leaders do seem to understand that deterrence 'works', or discouraged that they appear determined, *despite this understanding*, to press on with the acquisition of war-fighting capabilities, even though they judge the likelihood of nuclear war to be extremely low. But surely it is incorrect to claim that the 'stability of deterrence, in the Soviet conception, is directly proportional to the military's ability to prevail in war'.[74] It is both too 'hawkish' (in regard to Soviet military thinking), and too 'dovish' (in regard to the Soviet political system) in its assessment. Soviet leaders are able to understand deterrence as it is understood in the West; what they are not able, or at least not willing, to do is to accept mutual deterrence as a desirable and permanent state of affairs. They seek a war-fighting capability not because they identify deterrence with war-fighting, but rather because they remain fascinated by war-fighting.

In order to assess the prospects for a change in Soviet thinking in the direction of a more 'mutual' conception of security, it is necessary to explore those features of the Soviet system which account for the apparent drive to 'maximize' the level of security. Does Marxism-Leninism – in either its ideological or its organizational aspects – account for the Soviet Union's difficulty in accepting a purely deterrent relationship with the United States? And what accounts for the seeming political vulnerability of Soviet leaders who have tended in this direction?

Marxism-Leninism and doctrine
The impact of Marxism-Leninism on Soviet doctrine can be considered on three levels. The first relates to the conventions of language as they are used in the Soviet Union. Both Soviet and Western scholars agree that terms like 'war', 'peace' and 'aggression' have radically different meanings in Marxist and non-Marxist contexts.[75] In general, knowing Marxist-Leninist terminology is more useful for determining what doctrine does *not* say than for what it does. The flexibility of Marxist-Leninist terminology enables Soviet doctrine to gloss over many apparent inconsistencies (e.g. the difference between pre-emptive and preventive war).

The second level on which Marxism-Leninism can be considered is as a body of precepts handed down from one generation to another of Soviet leaders. Nathan Leites' 'operational code' studies concentrate on this level, as do many 'quotation-mongering' approaches to Soviet doctrine.[76] With their habit of applying Lenin's aphorisms to everyday problems, Soviet writers themselves tend to encourage an image of Marxism-Leninism as a 'handbook', a tactical guide to action. Not surprisingly, one may read in Western analyses that Lenin taught the importance of surprise, hence Soviet leaders are preoccupied with surprise attack in nuclear war, or that the Bolsheviks stressed the importance of the 'main blow', hence Khrushchev's fondness for strategic rocket attacks.[77] Unfortunately, Lenin's statements and 'laws' are so truistic (and so voluminous) that they lend themselves readily to *ex post facto* justification of policies which have already been selected by other criteria and are thus of little value in identifying precisely what these criteria might be.

The third (and for the purposes of research potentially most fruitful) level on which Marxism-Leninism can be considered is in regard to its impact on the 'strategic culture' or 'national style' of the Soviet Union.[78] Rather than focusing on Leninism as a 'code' which merely supplies answers to problems, this approach treats ideology as a total system of thought that defines the very nature of what constitutes a problem. More importantly, concepts such as 'strategic culture' are broad enough to account not only for the impact of written texts (e.g. the works of Lenin), but to encompass the organizational aspects of Communism as well. 'Strategic culture', in other words, is determined not only by the books that cadres read in Party schools, but by the entire pattern of political behaviour in the Soviet system.

The Soviet strategic culture

In examining the Soviet 'strategic culture', one should recognize that Marxism-Leninism is an essentially 'Utopian' system of thought, albeit of a peculiar sort. Utopias, moreover, are inherently 'maximalist' in their objectives. Western analysts often state or imply that, because Soviet reality has failed to live up to the original Utopian expectations of Marx and Lenin, and because world-wide 'Proletarian Revolution' has not materialized, ideology must be a spent or a dying force in the Soviet Union. With the 'failure' of certain basic predictions, a vast dissonance has been created between the 'official' view of the world propounded by the Party and 'reality' as it would be recognized by an outside observer. The West also tends to attribute the persistence of this dissonance either to self-delusion, or, more frequently, to cynicism and hypocrisy. Since there is obviously a disparity between ideology and reality, Western thinking suggests that a Communist either knows that his ideology is false and will not admit it (in which case he is a cynic), or he is incapable of recognizing reality (in which case he is deluded). What this assessment overlooks, however, is the fact that, as a Utopian system of thought, Marxism-Leninism is itself premised upon a certain gap between ideology and reality. The 'historic mission' of the Party – upon which it bases its ultimate legitimacy – is to overcome the reality-ideology gap. In a sense, the very 'falsity' of the ideology defines the day-to-day 'tasks' of the Party.

Unlike religious and philosophical Utopias, which generally transcend history,[79] the Soviet Utopia is immanent in history: it will be realized by the cumulative solution of a series of concrete 'tasks' which history sets for the Party and which the Party is capable of fulfilling. If there is a transcendent element in Soviet ideology, it manifests itself in the growing propensity to endow the Party itself with a quasi-religious, transcendent significance (one that derives from the *origins* of the Party – 'October' rather than from the *end-point* of the Party's work – Communist Utopia).[80] The peculiar brand of Utopianism embodied in Marxism-Leninism has a dual effect on Soviet strategic doctrine. On the one hand, as noted above, the very fact that Leninism is Utopian allows the system to tolerate a certain gap between declared doctrine and reality. The tendency of Soviet military doctrine to blur the distinction between intentions (or 'inevitabilities') and capabilities simply carries over from the general ideological framework. Soviet claims about the inevitability of victory in a nuclear war are voiced with perhaps no greater confidence than are statements about the fulfilment of other historic 'tasks' on the Party's agenda: the eradication of religion, nationalism, crime and disease; the transformation of human nature into 'new socialist man'; and the 'drawing together' and 'fusion' of nationalities. Such statements reflect *intent* rather than capability. On the other hand, while this ideology/reality gap is 'tolerated', at the same time there are constant pressures in the system to narrow this gap.

Continued pressure towards the fulfilment of this and other 'Utopian' tasks derive not only from the content of Soviet ideology, but from the organizational nature of the Soviet system. The Soviet Union remains a 'mobilizational' political system. At home, the Party seeks to maintain vigilance and to extract sacrifices from the population in the name of defending peace. Abroad, the cutting edge of Soviet diplomacy remains a 'peace policy', which is premised on the view that imperialism is warlike and that a natural alliance exists between the Soviet Union and all those who desire peace. As noted above, since 1956 Soviet leaders have carefully preserved an ambiguity in their assessments of the possibilities for nuclear war – of imperialist attack – in order to manipulate the war danger to mobilize domestic and international support. Seen in this light, it is hard to envisage what American actions short of, or perhaps even including, unilateral disarmament would allow the Soviet Union to believe that it had achieved a satisfactory level of security.

The imperatives of ideology, and more importantly, the organizational nature of the Soviet system itself and the distribution of power within it suggest that any regime will continually seek absolute security by minimizing, indeed eliminating altogether, Soviet dependence on deterministic elements. Deterrence, in that it gives the USSR some control over US actions, represented a dramatic shift away from the passive reliance on deterministic factors and towards a greater control over the Soviet Union's own destiny. At best, however, deterrence could be acknowledged as only a stopping point on a continuum towards an even greater level of security.

Maximizing Soviet security

The success or failure of the Soviet Union in fulfilling its long-term, maximal ambitions for attaining a war-winning capability will obviously be decided on the basis of a combination of its own unilateral efforts and by the corresponding actions of its principal strategic competitor, the United States. The scope of Soviet efforts will be determined in turn by the overall size and strength of the Soviet economy and by the willingness of the Soviet leadership to forego industrial investment, foreign aid, improvements in living standards and other economic objectives in order to allocate resources to the (virtually unlimited) requirements of a nuclear war-fighting strategy. In view of the continuing American determination to maintain a stable deterrent, the current Soviet leadership probably sees little likelihood of the USSR achieving, by such unilateral efforts alone, a level of absolute security *vis-à-vis* the United States. At least for the time being Soviet leaders recognize their dependence on both voluntaristic and deterministic factors in maintaining Soviet security, even though they are generally willing to acknowledge the latter only in retrospect. While vigorous Soviet defence efforts concentrate on unilaterally enhancing security – first-strike counterforce weapons, air defence, civil defence, research on ABM, space systems, and 'exotic' weapons – Soviet leaders seem less sanguine about the prospects for achieving a war-fighting capability than they were in the 1950s and 1960s. The reasons for this are two-fold: first, war-fighting has become an intrinsically more difficult problem with the proliferation of new systems (submarines, cruise missiles, etc.); and, second, the Soviet Union has failed to outstrip the US economically and technologically, as Khrushchev had expected.

In addition to these unilateral efforts, however, Soviet pursuit of 'absolute security' can be furthered by gaining some leverage over US policy. To the extent that the USSR utilizes arms control, propaganda, deception and disinformation to constrain US defence efforts, it can reduce the American threat to finite and stable dimensions and thus lessen the costs of acquiring a war-winning capability. In effect, propaganda, deception and other non-military means of constraining US defence efforts expand the USSR's 'unilateral' control over its destiny, using political and organizational resources rather than economic, scientific, technological and ultimately military means. Indeed, some observers have argued that the Soviet Union signed the ABM Treaty of 1972 precisely because it prevented the US from deploying a sophisticated ABM system and thus preserved the USSR's minimum security requirement – its deterrent – and enhanced the long-term prospects for the achievement of the maximum security which would be afforded by an effective first-strike capability.[81]

Unfortunately for Soviet planners, however, the very steps needed – at the level of both doctrine and force procurement – to maximize the military side of the Soviet quest for security are also those which, by raising US suspicions, hinder the effectiveness of non-military means to constrain US counter-efforts. Ironically, the dilemma faced by the USSR since the late 1970s is the reverse of that which Talenskii and his colleagues encountered in the early 1950s. The deterrent and political aspects of Stalin's doctrine precluded the emergence of an effective war-fighting strategy. In contrast, by the late 1970s the emphasis in Soviet military writings on war-fighting and the acquisition of counterforce capabilities undermined the political effectiveness of Soviet doctrine (arms control and the 'peace policy'). To the extent that, as a consequence, the US sought to achieve highly accurate and potential 'first strike' weapons, the deterrent value of Soviet forces was reduced as well.

The early 1970s marked a period in which the USSR did not have to make stringent choices between concentration on minimum and maximum security requirements. The Soviet deterrent was secure – indeed a key objective of US arms controllers was to assure its security – and the Soviet Union was successfully integrating the military and political elements in doctrine by claiming that strategic parity implied a Soviet right to 'equal security' and that 'equal security' in turn entailed wide-ranging political changes. Finally, the Soviet military was attempting to perfect its war-fighting capabilities, not with any spectacular success, but, by the same token, without provoking threatening American counter-efforts. By the late 1970s, however, the USSR once again had to choose between accentuating minimum and maximum elements in its doctrine. The war-fighting elements in Soviet doctrine were coming under increasing scrutiny in the US, and, with detente in ruins, there was reason to question the effectiveness of Soviet political strategy. Having reached strategic parity with the United States, the USSR was also at a point where continued increases in Soviet security would be small and bought at increasing cost.

Soviet institutions: division of labour or difference of opinion?
In the light of these difficulties it is worth asking whether there is any serious consideration in the Soviet Union of falling back to a less ambitious security policy. As noted previously, wrangling in the top leadership has occurred with General Ogarkov (when still Chief of the Soviet General Staff) stressing the war danger and calling for new capabilities to meet it and with other Soviet leaders seeming to resist his interpretation.

This recent controversy recalls the long-standing speculation in the West about whether there is a debate in the Soviet Union on the fundamentals of nuclear doctrine and strategy. According to one viewpoint, the military and selected allies (heavy industry, the KGB, the party ideologues) remain wedded to traditional concepts of war-fighting, while the Foreign Ministry, the Institute for the Study of World Politics and Economy (IMEMO), the Institute for the Study of the United States and Canada (also known as the USA Institute) and others are more sympathetic to Western ideas of deterrence based on mutual vulnerabilities.[82] Another Western view is more sceptical about the existence of a debate involving a so-called 'Arbatov tendency' (named after Georgi Arbatov, Head of the USA Institute) and suspects that the foreign policy institutes under the Academy of Sciences are engaged in a centrally-directed effort to mislead Western audiences.[83]

The question of whether such a debate exists in the Soviet Union is fundamental, but not easily resolved. From the standpoint of Soviet self-interest, those factors (i.e., the enormous economic and political costs) which would encourage a re-examination of a war-fighting doctrine are the very factors which analysts would expect the Soviet Union to play down in the hope of lowering these costs by gaining some control over Western policy. Thus it is impossible to decide whether there is such a debate solely on the basis of Soviet 'interests'.

An alternative approach is to undertake detailed Sovietological research to distinguish the roles of various institutions in the Soviet system. The question of whether or not there is a strategic debate in the Soviet Union is in fact only a special case of the more general question which all Sovietologists who rely on published Soviet sources must confront. Namely, do published Soviet sources serve as fora for the expression of the 'interests' of the bureaucratic bodies responsible for their production? Or do they reflect one over-riding and centrally-determined point of view which is then tailored to influence particular audiences? Does the newspaper *Trud*, for example, express the autonomous or partially autonomous view of Soviet trade unions? Or does it present merely the views of the Politburo in a form which is likely to appeal to Soviet trade union members and officials? At issue is whether differences in the content of various Soviet publications, insofar as they are systematic and not the product of mere chance, are attributable to genuine differences of opinion or to a division of labour. While there is probably no definitive answer to this question, clues about how certain communications should be treated can be obtained from what is known about the Soviet system. The time has long passed – if indeed there ever was such a time – when Sovietologists could indiscriminately treat every published statement or article in the Soviet press as a reflection of official Government policy. At the same time, however, there is as yet little to indicate that the USSR has become the kind of 'pluralist' system in which statements from different sources can be interpreted as more or less straightforward explications of the views or interests of various institutions. The picture is far more mixed.

In recent years, Western Sovietologists have produced detailed studies on the role of different institutions in the Soviet system. Timothy Colton's study of the Main Political Administration (MPA) of the Soviet Armed Forces has shed new light on the relationship between the Party and the military, and has demonstrated that Party-military conflict may be less acute than once was thought.[84] Oded Eran's study of the *mezhdunarodniki* has clarified the origins and role of the Soviet foreign policy research institutes and of IMEMO in particular.[85] At the Rand Corporation, studies based on interviews with émigrés have concentrated on the role of the media in the Soviet polity and have attempted to distinguish the various tasks assigned to (or the various interests expressed by) the different publications.[86] Although there is clearly scope for many more such studies, a composite picture of the Soviet system and of its defence and foreign policy establishments is gradually emerging. This picture is enriched by other research into the role of specialized technical knowledge and of a functional division of labour in the Soviet system.

In 1967 the Brezhnev regime initiated a major effort to revitalize Soviet ideology and to make it more responsive to the Party's need for Communists who would be both 'Red' and 'expert'. Brezhnev sought to overcome the traditional conflict between dogma and science by, in effect, 'rationalizing' ideology. Ideology began to display a more empiricist and positivist bent. Empirical sociology, for example, previously anathema from a dogmatic Marxist-Leninist viewpoint, was revived so that Party officials could use data from certain types of public opinion polling.[87] At the international level, there was a parallel effort to upgrade the use of specialized knowledge. The foundation of new international institutes, including Arbatov's USA Institute, stems from these 1967 decisions.

One objective of the post-1967 reform was to encourage the development of a new type of Communist professional and to build up a cadre of military officers, economists, political scientists and other specialists who both shared the goals of the Party leadership and who could hold their own in their increasingly frequent contacts with the West. This meant, at a minimum, increasing the immunity of Soviet experts to Western information. Maximally, it meant developing a body of skilled professionals who could communicate with and influence their Western professional counterparts. The so-called 'Arbatov tendency' should be viewed in the context of the new Soviet professionalism.

Rather than attempting to fit these 'civilian' specialists into a hypothetical 'debate' in the Soviet Union, in which men like Arbatov are alleged to be covertly challenging the Soviet General Staff, it may be more correct to view these people as specialists who, in keeping with the growing trend towards division of labour within the Soviet system, are concerned with the political implications of military developments rather than military development as such. Arbatov, for example, has for some years now been a leading exponent to Western audiences of the view that the relative decline of the United States in the military sphere must translate into the relative rise of the Soviet Union in the political sphere. Arbatov and his colleagues have inherited the task, begun by Khrushchev, of trying to acquire for the Soviet Union the equal (political) 'rights and opportunities' which flow from the attainment of strategic nuclear parity.

The hope that 'interest groups' such as the Foreign Ministry or the USA Institute are somehow emerging as voices of moderation in the Soviet system is probably illusory. Moreover, as this analysis has suggested, even if these groups were to voice such opposition, it would probably prove ineffective since they are generally far less powerful than the Soviet 'metal eaters' and their friends in the armed forces.

One should not rule out, however, the possibility of resistance to the open-ended claims of the armed forces. A more genuine and more effective source of opposition could be the general political executive. This could be identified variously as the General Secretary alone, the Politburo acting as a collective, or perhaps a key group within the Politburo. Less important than any precise definition is the fact that in the Soviet Union there is, presumably, a small, high-level group which must assess the overall allocation of resources to the various domestic and international objectives of the Soviet state. While in the West importance is often attached to whether the members of this group are civilians or military officers, moderates or hard-liners, these distinctions are probably less important than the 'generalist' responsibilities that fall to this group. There is little reason to expect that for reasons of ideological proclivity or career background a Khrushchev, a Brezhnev, or for that matter a Gorbachev would, as a matter of principle, argue against the need for a capability to win a nuclear war. On the contrary, the historical record seems to indicate that no Soviet official could reach the pinnacle of power if he advanced such an argument. In practice, however, as custodians of the Soviet state, these men have to decide whether the resources that would be needed to acquire such a capability might not be better spent elsewhere – for example in enhancing the Soviet Union's international economic stature or in 'building communism'.

The top leadership may indeed question the open-ended requirements of a war-fighting doctrine, whereas certain institutions will advance particularist claims which can be justified by the requirements of nuclear war-fighting. (Much as the US President and his Office of Management and Budget (OMB) are inevitably cast in the cost-cutting role *vis-à-vis* the specific interests represented in the Congress.) A key question for Western policy-makers is how, given a proper understanding of the workings of the Soviet system, they might encourage the 'general' political executive to exclude from the long-term goals of the Soviet Union the acquisition of war-fighting capabilities.

IV. CONCLUSIONS

This Paper has argued that the deterrence/war-fighting dichotomy which has structured Western analysis of Soviet doctrine is inadequate. Instead, it has suggested that Soviet leaders are concerned with both deterrence *and* war-fighting – the former 'a minimum', the latter a 'maximum' objective. The United States, after enjoying the maximum but transitory security afforded by an ability to fight and probably win a nuclear war, in large part came to accept that it would have to be content with some version of a minimum objective, namely a secure deterrent force. Maximum security was no longer attainable – at any cost. The Soviet Union, having achieved the minimum level of security afforded by a deterrent, seems determined, by devoting enormous sums to its military build-up, to achieve a maximum, indeed absolute, level of security.

This Paper has attempted to show the various forces which encourage policy-makers to pursue war-fighting doctrines and to acquire the capabilities necessary to support it. First, it has stressed that all theories of deterrence are inherently vulnerable to the 'what if it doesn't work?' argument. In the Soviet Union, this argument seems to carry special weight in light of the bleak view of the enemy prescribed by Marxism-Leninism. Assessments of the likelihood of war can thus be used to question the adequacy of virtually *any* defence posture, and particularly one geared solely to deterrence. Second, the nature of competition for power and resources in the Soviet system and the balance of domestic political forces encourages mobilization in favour of those particular interests identified with the war-fighting doctrine. Third, the nature of Soviet ideology, with its constant calls for the solution of 'impossible' tasks, provides an overall framework for and a predisposition towards the adoption of a war-fighting doctrine. Against this formidable array of pressures must be weighed the caution with which Soviet writers approach nuclear weapons and the practical problems which must be overcome in order to acquire a war-winning capability.

From the point of view of long-term prospects for peace and stability, both disturbing and faintly encouraging elements emerge from this analysis of Soviet doctrine. On the negative side, no Soviet leadership will surrender of its own volition the quest for a maximum level of security. The history of the post-Stalin period has shown repeatedly that any move towards acceptance of an exclusively deterrent posture automatically creates an issue around which the most powerful groups in the system (heavy industry, the armed forces, Party ideologues) can mobilize against the top leadership. Brezhnev's long tenure in office may attest to his understanding of this fundamental fact of Soviet politics and may account for the size of the claim on resources which the military enjoyed during the 1960s and 1970s.

On the slightly more promising side, one may conclude that, despite the pressures within the Soviet system militating against acceptance of deterrence, there are elements in the Soviet elite who do perceive the enormous cost associated with the alternative policy. While the hope that 'interest groups', such as the USA Institute or the Foreign Ministry, are emerging as voices of moderation in the Soviet system is probably ill-founded, a more effective source of resistance to the open-ended claims of the military may be what has been termed here the general political executive. This executive may decide that the overall interests of the Soviet state are not especially well-served by the pursuit of absolute security.

It is disturbing that, for whatever reasons, the top leadership of the past 15 years has identified the general interests of the Soviet state with continued high levels of military expenditure, and that, even in retrospect, it seems reasonably satisfied with the return on its investment. Soviet military power is credited with 'sobering' the US and compelling it to accept detente, with accelerating the rise of 'progressive' forces in the Third World, and generally with preserving world peace and hence permitting the continuation of Communist construction. At the same time, however, the Soviet leadership (and, indeed, the armed forces themselves) are frustrated by the Soviet inability to resolve decisively the maximum security problem. Assured destruction remains an unpleasant fact of life. Moreover, the prospects for an early breakthrough in this area do not appear promising. Soviet economic resources are stretched, the US will deploy new systems to preserve its deterrent posture (at the least), and improvements in existing Soviet systems – such as air and missile defence – are likely to be bought at increasingly large costs.

The recent controversy in the West about what Soviet doctrine 'really' says, or whether this doctrine is changing has focused on the wrong issue. While Soviet doctrine clearly calls for the Soviet military to 'solve' the problem of fighting and winning a nuclear war, such calls should be viewed in the overall context of the Soviet system. By its very nature this system sets itself impossible tasks – the eradication of nationalism, the building of a Utopia, and the achievement of absolute security. To search for signs that the Soviet Union has abandoned or is about to abandon its long-term attempts to resolve these problems is probably fruitless. By the same token, however, the Soviet Union, with its existing constrained resources, cannot pursue all its long-term ambitions with equal vigour. Western scholarship should focus on identifying the *relative* priority assigned by the elite to the fulfilment of these various tasks. Western policy might also attempt to influence the Soviet Union so that the Government devotes less of its resources to achieving a war-winning capability.

The least sensible approach for US policy-makers to adopt is one based on the assumption that the Soviet Union, rather than being burdened by its ideology and its impossible pretensions, is somehow possessed of superior wisdom and insight, and that the US should mimic the USSR by plunging into an open-ended race to achieve societal invulnerability and the ability to wage protracted nuclear war. Equally lacking in sense is a policy premised on the assumption that unilateral restraint by the US and a 'dialogue' with the Soviet Union on strategic matters can convince the Soviet leadership that attaining absolute security is undesirable. US restraint would merely simplify the problem for the Soviet Union. By solving its minimum security problem, the US would simply allow the Soviet Union a free hand in devoting its efforts to a long-term achievement of its maximum security ambitions. Moreover, to the extent that the Soviet leaders came to believe that the US was 'compelled' to exercise restraint and to enter into arms-control talks, US policy would encourage the Soviet Union to exert a still greater degree of control over US security policy and thus encourage Soviet long-term hopes for the achievement of absolute security.

If the US ought not to mimic blindly the Soviet effort to achieve a war-winning capability, nor persist in – or rather return to – the policies of the early 1970s, what course is open? It might begin by adopting its own minimum and maximum security objectives. Its minimum objective must be to preserve a secure deterrent. Unlike the Soviet Union, however, the US should not adopt a programme to achieve absolute security through a war-winning capability. Rather, its maximum security objective should be to encourage the Soviet Union, if not to abandon its pursuit of absolute security, at least to realize that the continued pursuit of this objective will prove so expensive that it will undermine virtually every other domestic and foreign policy objective that the Soviet leadership might hope to pursue. In short, the US should adopt policies to discourage Soviet efforts to escape unilaterally the logic of the nuclear stalemate.

In this regard, the Reagan Administration's plans to make obsolete large portions of the past Soviet defence effort, to the extent that they are successful, could prove stabilizing rather than, as some critics fear, destabilizing. Such plans may remove Soviet incentives to seek to achieve invulnerability in the face of the US nuclear deterrent.[88] Conversely, the efforts of the early 1970s, driven by the needs of arms control, to achieve strategic stability by restraining US counterforce and damage limitation efforts may have been counterproductive, in that they encouraged the Soviet military to believe that, with continued exertions, the USSR could achieve some ultimately 'destabilizing' breakthrough towards a state of absolute security. By the same token, however, arms control should not be dismissed as an instrument to ensure Western security. Using arms control in the early 1970s to 'educate' the USSR into accepting a new and less ambitious military doctrine was misdirected, not so much in terms of the objective so much as in the means by which the US sought to realize this objective. It is possible that a combination of American military effort, coupled with arms-control talks with the Soviet Union, could lead to some evolution in Soviet thinking about nuclear matters, although it must be said that, for the time being at least, the Soviet Union seems not prepared to co-operate in such a dialogue.

Perhaps the most important lesson to be learned from this analysis of Soviet doctrine concerns the political and not the strictly military aspects of policy towards the Soviet Union. In spite of the vagaries of the US-

Soviet rivalry since 1945, and all the technical complexities of the nuclear competition itself, the advice offered by George Kennan in his 1947 article 'The Sources of Soviet Conduct' remains valid.[89] Kennan focused on the gap between Soviet intentions and capabilities (much as this Paper has done) and cautioned Western leaders that they could neither afford to ignore the intentions, nor confuse these intentions with reality itself. He argued that the USSR was indeed governed by certain 'messianic' ambitions which the West, with its superior resources, could frustrate or 'contain'. If these ambitions were frustrated for a sufficient period, Kennan hoped that Soviet leaders would come to recognize the widening gap between their ideological pretensions and reality. Recognition of this gap might lead to a fundamental rethinking in the Soviet Union of its relationship with the West.

In retrospect Kennan's analysis appears overly optimistic. In particular, he grossly underestimated the self-confirming nature of ideology, especially an ideology in the hands of a powerful Party commanding the resources of a powerful state. This self-confirming role presents Western policy-makers with a major dilemma. On the one hand, Western restraint and policies of detente are interpreted, as recent years have shown, to mean that the USSR is 'gaining' on its rivals and that the reality-ideology gap is steadily narrowing. On the other hand, Western assertiveness and efforts to contain the USSR simply 'prove' the fundamentally aggressive nature of the Soviet Union's rivals and thus justify calls for greater exertions in the USSR. Western policy cannot easily remedy this dilemma, since it derives from the essential solipsism of Marxist-Leninist thought. At a minimum, however, Western leaders can, as Kennan urged repeatedly, remain clear in their own minds about the difference between the 'real' world and the world created by Marxism-Leninism. In the field of nuclear weapons and nuclear war-fighting, this difference is by no means trivial.

Notes

[1] *Soviet Military Power* (Washington DC: USGPO, 1981), p. 54.
[2] *The Threat to Europe* (Moscow: Progress Publishers, 1981) p. 11; *Whence the Threat to Peace* (Moscow: Military Publishing House, 1982), pp. 58–62. In July 1982, the Soviet Ministry of Defence issued a second edition of the latter document, in which there was an expanded section on US doctrine.
[3] Tass, 15 June 1982.
[4] Fritz Ermarth, 'Contrasts in American and Soviet Strategic Thought', *International Security*, Fall 1978, vol. 3, no. 2; Benjamin Lambeth, *How to Think about Soviet Military Doctrine* (Santa Monica, CA: Rand, February 1978, P-5939); Richard Pipes, 'Why the Soviet Union Thinks It Could Fight and Win a Nuclear War', *Commentary*, July 1977, vol. 64, no. 1.
[5] Raymond Garthoff, 'Mutual Deterrence and Strategic Arms Limitation in Soviet Policy', *International Security*, Summer 1978, vol. 3, no. 1. See also Mason Willrich, 'SALT I: An Appraisal', in Willrich and John B. Rhinelander (eds.), *SALT: The Moscow Agreements and Beyond* (New York: The Free Press, 1974).
[6] For a useful overview of this debate, with thorough documentation, see the editors' introduction to J. Baylis and G. Segal (eds.), *Soviet Strategy* (London: Croom Helm, 1981). See also William F. Scott, *Soviet Sources of Military Doctrine and Strategy* (New York: Crane, Russak & Company, 1975).
[7] For the evolution of Robert McNamara's views, see Lawrence Freedman, *The Evolution of Nuclear Strategy* (London: Macmillan, 1981), pp. 225–56.
[8] *US Foreign Policy for the 1970s: A New Strategy for Peace*, 18 February 1970, p. 92. Even Nixon's rejection of MAD was misleading in that it caricatured the 'assured destruction' doctrine of McNamara into something it was not.
[9] Benjamin Lambeth, *Selective Nuclear Options in American and Soviet Strategic Policy* (Santa Monica, CA: Rand, December 1976, R-2034-DDRE).
[10] For the Carter Administration, see Walter Slocombe, 'The Countervailing Strategy', *International Security*, Spring 1981, vol. 5, no. 4; for the Reagan Administration, see Richard Halloran, 'Pentagon Draws Up First Strategy for Fighting a Long Nuclear War', *New York Times*, 30 May 1982.
[11] Colin S. Gray, 'National Style in Strategy: The American Example', *International Security*, Fall 1981, vol. 6, no. 2, p. 42.
[12] Quoted in Herbert S. Dinerstein, *War and the Soviet Union* (New York: Praeger Publishers, 1959), p. 69.
[13] *Ibid.*, p. 71.
[14] See Earl C. Ravenal, 'Counterforce and Alliance: The Ultimate Connection', *International Security*, Spring 1982, vol. 6, no. 4.
[15] Thomas W. Wolfe, *The SALT Experience: Its Impact on U.S. and Soviet Strategic Policy and Decisionmaking* (Santa Monica, CA: Rand, September 1975, R-1686-PR), pp. 118–9
[16] Gray (*op. cit.* in note 11); Jack Snyder, *The Soviet Strategic Culture: Implications for Limited Nuclear Options* (Santa Monica, CA: Rand, September 1977, R-2154-AF).
[17] V.D. Sokolovskii (ed.), *Soviet Military Strategy*, (Englewood Cliffs, NJ: Prentice-Hall-Rand, 1963), translated with an introduction by Herbert S. Dinerstein, Leon Gouré and Thomas W. Wolfe, p. 314.
[18] The most prominent example is the debate over the Soviet threat to the US *Minuteman* force.
[19] A good discussion of the Soviet definition of doctrine is in William R. Kintner and Harriet Fast Scott, *Soviet Military Affairs* (Norman: University of Oklahoma Press, 1968), p. 6.
[20] Major General I. Sidelnikov, 'To Whom and For What Is Military Superiority Necessary', *Krasnaia zvezda*, 15 January 1980. See also Henry Trofimenko, 'The "Theology" of Strategy', *Orbis*, Fall 1977, vol. 21, no. 3.
[21] *Pravda*, 12 July 1982.
[22] This view is taken, for example, by Stanley Sienkiewicz, 'Soviet Nuclear Doctrine and Prospects for Strategic Arms Control', in Derek Leebaert (ed.), *Soviet Military Thinking* (Boston: Allen & Unwin, 1981), p. 81.

23 Arnold L. Horelick and Myron Rush, *Strategic Power and Soviet Foreign Policy* (Chicago: University of Chicago Press, 1966).
24 George H. Quester, 'On the Identification of Real and Pretended Communist Military Doctrine', *Journal of Conflict Resolution*, June 1966, vol. 10, no. 2, pp. 172–9.
25 Dinerstein (*op. cit.* in note 12), p. 177.
26 Milovan Djilas, *Conversations with Stalin* (New York: Harcourt Brace, 1962).
27 See, for example, his conversation with the British ambassador to the USSR, Sir Frank Roberts, reported by Joseph Alsop in *Washington Post*, 12 July 1961, and quoted in Robert M. Slusser, *The Berlin Crisis of 1961* (Baltimore: Johns Hopkins University Press, 1973), pp. 43–4.
28 By 1963, Soviet writers, including the authors of the second edition of Sokolovskii, were playing down the intercontinental counterforce mission. See Mark E. Miller, *Soviet Strategic Power and Doctrine: The Quest for Superiority* (Miami: University of Miami Center for Advanced International Studies, 1981) p. 55.
29 See, for example, N. Talenskii, 'Anti-Missile Systems and Disarmament', *International Affairs*, October 1964, pp. 15–19.
30 P.H. Vigor, *The Soviet View of War, Peace and Neutrality* (London: Routledge & Kegan Paul, 1975).
31 Desmond Ball, *Can Nuclear War Be Controlled?*, Adelphi Papers no. 169 (London: IISS, 1981).
32 Jeff McCausland, 'The SS-20: Military and Political Threat?', *The Fletcher Forum*, Winter 1982, vol. 6, no. 1, p. 15.
33 Carl H. Builder, *The Case for First Strike Counterforce Capability* (Santa Monica, CA: Rand, July 1978, P-6179); and Victor Utgoff, 'In Defense of Counterforce', *International Security*, Spring 1982, vol. 6, no. 4.
34 See Fritz W. Ermarth, *Internationalism, Security, and Legitimacy: The Challenge to Soviet Interests in East Europe, 1964–1968* (Santa Monica, CA: Rand, March 1969, RM-5909-PR).
35 Quoted in Horelick and Rush (*op. cit.* in note 23), pp. 87–8.
36 Freedman (*op. cit.* in note 7), p. 238.
37 Lambeth (*op. cit.* in note 9), p. 11.
38 Horelick and Rush (*op. cit.* in note 23), p. 69. Even Miller (*op. cit.* in note 28, p. 56), who argues that early technical difficulties in the Soviet missiles played as large a part as deliberate restraint in limiting the Soviet ICBM effort, concludes that: for 'all the considerable operational deficiencies of the first and second generation ICBMs and Khrushchev's concern with cost-effectiveness, it is improbable that these factors alone were sufficient to preclude rapid, large-scale deployment. Had the Soviets estimated the likelihood of war as very great, they almost assuredly would have sought to maximize their strategic striking power as quickly as possible'.
39 Horelick and Rush (*op. cit.* in note 23), pp. 108–9.
40 Dinerstein (*op. cit.* in note 12), p. 18.
41 *Ibid.*, p. 154.
42 *Ibid.*, p. 93.
43 *Ibid.*, p. 163.
44 Discussion of the importance of this speech appears in the introduction to the Rand edition of Sokolovskii, *Soviet Military Strategy* (*op. cit.* in note 17), p. 14 ff.
45 *Pravda*, 25 October 1961.
46 B. Ponomarev, A. Gromyko, V. Khvostov, *History of Soviet Foreign Policy*, vol. 2 (1945–70) (Moscow: Progress Publishers, 1974), p. 514.
47 See, for example, 'Khrushchov [sic] Replies to Questions Submitted by P. Dampson', reprinted in *International Affairs*, November 1957, no. 11.
48 Excerpts of Brezhnev's speech appear in *Survival*, June 1966, vol. 8, no. 6, p. 200.
49 Quoted in Miller (*op. cit.* in note 28), p. 187.
50 Gail Warshofsky Lapidus, 'The Brezhnev Regime and Directed Social Change: Depoliticization as Political Strategy', in Alexander Dallin (ed.), *The Twenty-Fifth Congress of the CPSU* (Stanford: Hoover Institution, 1977).
51 See the Brezhnev UN message, Tass, 15 June 1982.
52 *Kommunist*, July 1981.
53 N.V. Ogarkov, *Vsegda v gotovnosti k zashchite otechestva* [*Always in Readiness to Defend the Homeland*] (Moscow: Ministry of Defence, 1982).
54 Quoted in Dinerstein (*op. cit.* in note 12), p. 6.
55 *Ibid.*
56 Major General Talenskii, 'On the

Question of the Laws of Military Science', *Military Thought*, September 1953.

[57] Dinerstein (*op. cit.* in note 12); and Raymond Garthoff, *Soviet Military Policy* (London: Faber & Faber, 1966).

[58] In the first of these periods, 'Soviet military strategy was being developed on the basis of the rich experience of the Great Fatherland War, but when at the same time the presence of nuclear weapons in the US was taken into consideration . . .' In the second period, military strategy became concerned with 'the introduction of nuclear weapons and missiles into the Armed Forces and the emergence of new armed services and troop branches', *Soviet Military Encyclopedia*, excerpts translated in *Strategic Review*, Spring 1980, vol. 8, no. 2.

[59] *Ibid.*

[60] See, for example, Miller (*op. cit.* in note 28), who makes a compelling case that the Soviet military has always sought to acquire the capabilities to enable it to win a nuclear war.

[61] 'As for the military bases in Europe, Africa and Asia, missiles which can reach any part of these continents have already been in existence for a long time. I think it is no secret that there now exists a range of missiles with the aid of which it is possible to fulfil any assignment of operational and strategic importance . . . . Can it be supposed that military bases are known only to those who established them? But if their location is known, then, given the present level of missile and other technology, they can speedily be rendered ineffective'. 'Khrushchov [sic] Replies to Questions Submitted by P. Dampson' (*op. cit.* in note 47), p. 15.

[62] Comments by US Secretary of Defense Harold Brown at US Naval Academy commencement ceremonies, reported in the *New York Times*, 31 May 1979, and cited in John M. Collins, *US–Soviet Military Balance: Concepts and Capabilities* (New York: McGraw-Hill, 1980), p. 118.

[63] Admiral S.G. Gorshkov, *The Sea Power of the State* (Oxford: Pergamon Press, 1979), p. x; Michael MccGwire, 'Soviet Naval Doctrine and Strategy', in Leebaert (ed.) (*op. cit.* in note 22), pp. 150–54.

[64] Sokolovskii, *Soviet Military Strategy* (3rd edition), edited by Harriet Fast Scott (London: Macdonald and Jane's, 1968), pp. 283–4.

[65] *Ibid.*

[66] See also Robert Lee Arnett, 'Soviet Attitudes towards Nuclear War Survival (1962-1967): Has There Been a Change?' Unpublished Ph.D. dissertation, Ohio State University, 1979.

[67] *Pravda*, 30 March 1966.

[68] Thomas W. Wolfe, *Soviet Power and Europe* (Baltimore: Johns Hopkins University Press, 1970), p. 441.

[69] *Ibid.*, pp. 454–5.

[70] Thomas W. Wolfe, *Military Power and Soviet Policy* (Santa Monica, CA: Rand, March 1975, P-5388), p. 18.

[71] Ponomarev, *et.al.* (*op. cit.* in note 46), p. 118.

[72] *Ibid.*, p. 118.

[73] *Ibid.*, p. 417.

[74] Miller (*op. cit.* in note 28), p. 32.

[75] General discussion of Marxist terminology is offered by P.H. Vigor (*op. cit.* in note 30).

[76] Nathan Leites, *A Study of Bolshevism* (Glencoe, IL.: The Free Press, 1953).

[77] Other analysts trace Soviet strategic thought to Russian history and the Tsarist military tradition. See, for example, Rebecca V. Strode and Colin S. Gray, 'The Imperial Dimension of Soviet Military Power', *Problems of Communism*, Nov/Dec. 1981, vol. 30, no. 6.

[78] See Gray (*op. cit.* in note 11); and Snyder, (*op. cit.* in note 16).

[79] Examples would be the Garden of Eden, the Christian millenium and Rousseau's 'state of nature'.

[80] As Andropov stated in his 1982 Lenin Anniversary Speech, 'The victory of Great October, at the source of which was Lenin, as it were disrupted the common flow of historical time'. Moscow home service, 22 April 1982, reported in BBC *Summary of World Broadcasts*, 24 April 1982.

[81] Wolfe (*op. cit.* in note 15), p. 118.

[82] Dennis Ross, 'Rethinking Soviet Strategic Policy: Inputs and Implications', in Baylis and Segal (*op. cit.* in note 6), pp. 134–5

[83] Harry Gelman, *The Politburo's Management of Its America Problem* (Santa Monica, CA: Rand, April 1981, R-2707-NA), p. 50.

[84] Timothy J. Colton, *Commissars, Commanders, and Civilian Authority: The Structure of Soviet Military Politics*, (Cambridge, MA: Harvard University Press, 1979).

[85] Oded Eran, *The Mezhdunarodniki: An Assessment of Professional Expertise in the Making of Soviet Foreign Policy* (Ramat Gan: Turtledove Publishing, 1979).
[86] Lilita Dzirkals, Thane Grustafson and A. Ross Johnson, *The Media and Intra-Elite Communications in the USSR* (Santa Monica, CA: Rand, September 1982, R-2869).
[87] For a good discussion of ideological change under Brezhnev and the implications for the professions, see Frederick C. Barghoorn, *Politics in the USSR* (Boston: Little, Brown, 1972), p. 94 ff.
[88] Halloran (*op. cit.* in note 10).
[89] George Kennan ('X'), 'The Sources of Soviet Conduct', *Foreign Affairs*, July 1947, vol. 25, no. 4, pp. 466–82.